Rosemary

This script is published by
DCG Publications.

All inquiries regarding purchase of further scripts and current royalty rates should be addressed to:

DCG Media Group
Vamos 73008
Chania
Crete
Greece

Email: info@dcgmediagroup.com
www.dcgmediagroup.com

Conditions

- ❖ All DCG Publication scripts are fully protected by the copyright acts. Under no circumstances must they be reproduced by photo-copying or any other means, either in whole or in part.

- ❖ The license to perform referred to above only relates to live performances of this script. A separate license is required for video-taping or sound recording, which will be issued on receipt of the appropriate fee.

- ❖ The name of the author shall be clearly stated on all publicity, programs etc. The program credits shall state "Script provided by DCG Publications".

Rosemary

By
Glyn Jones

DCG
Publicatio

First Published in Greece 2010

© Glyn Idris Jones
The author's moral rights have been asserted

DCG Publications
www.dcgmediagroup.com

ISBN 978-960-98418-8-7

Typeset by
DCG Publications

Printed in England by
Lightning Source.

For
Rosemary Matthews
Actress

Cast

Rosemary
Walter
Robert
Tracey
Matron

Time

1984 or thereabouts.

ACT ONE
SCENE ONE

Two entrances: one to the outside world, one to the rest of the home. There is the sound of a rackety slightly out of tune piano playing an old Music Hall song, possibly George Leybourne's "If Ever I Cease To Love." [1]

Part of the day-room of an old people's home. Parker-Knoll type chairs with easy remove covers, tables with wipe-down tops, institutional polyester curtains, plastic plants, everything sparse, clean, utilitarian.

MATRON enters, engrossed in examining one of a sheaf of papers she carries. She is half way across the room when one foot suddenly slides out from beneath her. She lets out a little cry and recovers her balance as one hand flies to her hip where she has obviously felt the spasm. She stands for a moment in order to regain her composure, then takes a closer look at the floor, turns back the way she has come and bellows.

MATRON: Robert? *(She waits.)* Robert!

ROBERT appears. He wears scuffed white shoes, jeans, and a not completely clean white jacket. MATRON glares at him.

Who polished this floor?

ROBERT: Polished?

MATRON: That's what I said.

ROBERT looks at the floor, back at MATRON, shrugs. TRACEY WILLIAMS appears behind ROBERT.

---

1 * Music available from DCG Publications.

MATRON: Nurse?

TRACEY: Matron?

ROBERT: She wants to know...

MATRON: SHE? Who is she? The cat's mother?

ROBERT: Matron wants to know who...

MATRON: Polished the floor.

ROBERT: Polished the floor.

TRACEY: Polished the floor?

MATRON: God give me patience. (*Her hand goes to her back where she feels another spasm. Gingerly she starts to lower herself into a chair, thinks better of it, and pushes herself up again.*) How many times do I have to say it? How many times? Clean floors but not polished floors! What are we trying to do? Send them off before their time?

ROBERT: When's their time?

MATRON: Thank you very much, we'll have less of that if you don't mind. Pick up those papers for me... (*Indicating some she dropped and then, remembering her manners*) ...please.

ROBERT does so and hands them to her as she continues.

And please don't tell me this floor hasn't been polished because I have just done a Torville and Dean.

ROBERT: Together? (*Seeing her look.*) Sorry.

MATRON: And all I want to say is, do you realise what a broken bone can mean in an elderly person? Do you want me to spell it out for you?

TRACEY: Matron, may I point out...

MATRON: No, you may not, not until I have finished.

TRACEY: We are not responsible for cleaning this place. The cleaning ladies are.

MATRON: Place? Place! This place?

TRACEY: Sorry, matron... Home... We're not res...

MATRON: (*Holding up an imperious hand.*) Perhaps not, nurse Williams, but we are all, every one of us who are employed here, responsible for the welfare of those entrusted to our charge and, the more frail and helpless they are, the more loving attention they need, and the more willingly we should give it. (*To ROBERT who is standing behind her back.*) And it's no good looking like that, Robert. I know you've heard me say it all before but it obviously didn't sink in. Do I have to think of everything? Supervise everything? How old are you, nurse?

TRACEY: Twenty.

MATRON: Then it's high time you learnt the meaning of the word responsibility. Even though a great many people don't seem to know the meaning of it these days.

She turns to look at ROBERT. He thinks about it and then, finally...

ROBERT: Twenty-three

MATRON: A third or more of your way through life. And,

> believe me, the other two thirds will fly by so fast, one day before you know it you may find yourself in a place like this.

TRACEY: Place?

MATRON: Home. (*To ROBERT.*) You were going to say something?

ROBERT: No.

MATRON: Oh yes you were. You were going to say "God forbid."

ROBERT shrugs.

> Well all I can say is, I hope you never have to suffer a shattered pelvis due to someone else's negligence.

ROBERT: They shouldn't slip, matron. Sticks and walking frames have rubber tips.

MATRON: Slippers do not have rubber tips. Slippers are called slippers not just because you slip into them but because you slip in them.

TRACEY starts to laugh. Stifles it.

> All right, so I made that up. But it also makes my point. Now please do something about this floor. (*She turns to go and finds herself face to face with ROBERT.*) I do wish you'd give up smoking, Robert.

MATRON sidesteps ROBERT and continues on her way. ROBERT gives a "what was all that about?" reaction to TRACEY and then watches MATRON until she has almost left before...

ROBERT: It's not polished.

MATRON freezes, slowly turns.

MATRON: I beg your pardon?

ROBERT: It's a patch of something... oil... or something.

MATRON returns. They all stand looking down at the floor. Finally...

MATRON: Then do something about it. (*She turns away again, talking as she goes.*) Oh, there's a new resident due. Call me when she arrives. Her name is Rosemary, Court of Protection.

And she has gone.

TRACEY: Oh, God! Another incontinent.

ROBERT: She'd make a great politician, that one. Just can't admit she's ever wrong. (*He takes hold of TRACEY and swings her over the oil patch.*) Shall we dance?

TRACEY: Stop it, Robert... Robert!

ROBERT: Trace... (*He tries to nuzzle into her neck.*)

TRACEY: Let me go please. Mrs Crabtree is watching.

ROBERT: I love you.

TRACEY: What! You have absolutely no conception of what that word means.

ROBERT: Maybe not. But I have every conception of what conception means.

TRACEY: Don't be smart with me, Robert Benham. Hadn't you better do something about that? (*Indicating the floor.*) Before matron gets back?

ROBERT: And hadn't you better get over to old mother Crabtree? She's waving at you with what passes as frantic in geriatric sign language. Or is it just a friendly hello? Or maybe a last good-bye.

TRACEY: (*Leaving.*) She probably wants to complain about your behaviour which doesn't surprise me.

ROBERT: I'm giving up this job.

TRACEY: Good.

ROBERT: I'm going to work in a holiday camp. At least there some of the people are alive... I think.

TRACEY has gone. He raises his voice to carry on talking to her.

Or maybe I'll get a job on a cruise liner. There the living dead are at least rich living dead.

WALTER appears carrying a tub of lavatory cleaner and a floor cloth. He stops when he sees ROBERT.

ROBERT: Talk about zombies and one will appear. Well, Walter? And what do you want? (*Silence.*) Well, come on, out with it. Figuratively speaking. You must want something. (*Silence.*) Cat's mother got your tongue? Wouldn't surprise me. She probably had it for breakfast pickled in acid. What's this? (*He takes the tub.*) Lavatory cleaner? You're going to clean the toilets are you?

WALTER shakes his head.

(*Smiling.*) Oh, what then? You're going to wash your head and flush it down the toilet.

WALTER: Floor.

ROBERT: What?

WALTER: Floor.

ROBERT: Floor? You're going to flush your head down the floor. That makes sense.

TRACEY returns.

What did old Mother C want?

TRACEY: She thought you were her son.

ROBERT: What!

TRACEY: Mrs Crabtree. Thought you were her son come to visit.

ROBERT: (*Not unsympathetically.*) What's she on about, poor old cow? Her son is part of the great American dream, tattered though it might be. She hasn't seen or heard of him in forty years. What makes her think she's going to hear from him now?

TRACEY: That's her dream, isn't it? To see him again before she... you know...

ROBERT: Pops her clogs. Fat chance. The only thing'll bring him back to visit the country of his birth is the sound of a lawyer reading her will. She's going to have to get by on faded memories and faded snapshots.

TRACEY continues on her way out.

TRACEY: She can dream can't she?

ROBERT: Why not? There's not much else for her to do. But it's what you're doing, Walter, me old china, that interests me. Now what is all this about?

WALTER: Floor. I've got to clean it. The floor.

ROBERT: Have you now? You don't mean the whole floor though, do you?

WALTER shakes his head.

You mean just a little bit here, don't you, my dear?

WALTER nods.

Just this teensy-weensy bit right here.

WALTER nods.

Because you've gone and spilt something all over it, Walter, my old darling, and got me into serious trouble with matron.

WALTER shakes his head violently.

Oh, yes, you have, Walter baby. No good gazing at me with those vacant china blue eyes. Now what was it you spilt over this nice clean floor?

WALTER: Oil! Oil! I didn't mean to do it, Mr Benham! Oil! I didn't mean to!

ROBERT: Did you not?

WALTER shakes his head.

Then what were you doing with the oil in the first place, Walter?

WALTER: It's for my wooood.

ROBERT: Your wooood? What wood? You have a wooden

	leg perhaps? I didn't know you had a wooden leg, Walter.
WALTER:	(*Looking down at his legs.*) When did that happen, Mr Benham?
ROBERT:	But oil's not what you want for a wooden leg, old son. No, worm exterminator is what you need for that.
WALTER:	Is it?
ROBERT:	Though you do have to be careful with it, Walter, because it could seep upwards in a capillary action and exterminate you as well, my little burnt-out schizo. Do you know what I'm talking about, Walter?

WALTER nods.

You do? Well isn't life just full of surprises? So what is this wooood you're on about, Walter?

WALTER:	Pear.
ROBERT:	Pair? Pair of what?
WALTER:	Not pair. Pear!
ROBERT:	Have you been studying Bhuddism in your spare time, Walt? Is this a Koan by which you expect me to achieve sudden enlightenment?

WALTER stares at him.

Perhaps, Walter, in your advanced years, after the days of your schizophrenic delusions, the torture those primitive medics put you through, and the agonies of your long life, you have attained a great wisdom. Pair. Maybe meditation on and the

	repetition of the word "pair," like that of the sacred word "Om" whilst contemplating my navel, will produce the answer to life's hidden mysteries.
WALTER:	What are you on about, you stupid young git? Don't you know what a pear is?
ROBERT:	My God! There's still fire in its belly. In its twisted entrails, its shrivelled testicles, there are yet signs of life. Can you still raise it, Walter, old son? Can the little man still stand proud and erect? Can you still sail a gravy boat on it?

He gives WALTER a prod. WALTER leaps back, slapping away the hand.

WALTER:	Keep your hands to yourself, you dirty little tyke.
ROBERT:	I bet you could have been a regular stud in your day, Walter, if you'd had the chance. No chance now though. Nothing left in your old age. Not even the thought of Mrs Palmer and her five children to bring you comfort.
WALTER:	(*With great dignity.*) Excuse me.

He tries to get by and down to clean the floor but ROBERT holds out an arm to stop him.

ROBERT:	Hold it right there. We still haven't solved the riddle of this pair. This pair of what?
WALTER:	(*Singing.*) On the first day of Christmas my true love gave to me...
ROBERT:	My God! This time he really has lost 'em.
WALTER:	...a partridge in a pear tree.
ROBERT:	Partridge.

WALTER: In a pear tree.

ROBERT: I heard you.

WALTER: But the tree's been chopped down. They chopped it down. No right. No right at all. Over a hundred years it was... old.

ROBERT: Almost as old as you, Walter.

WALTER: Pear. It's the best there is. For carving. End of the garden. They chopped it down. Next to lime, pear is best. Pear and lime are best.

ROBERT: And you have some lime as well do you, Walter?

WALTER: (*Nods.*) I wanted to rub some oil in so they don't dry out.

ROBERT: Walter, my heart, they've already dried out. Like sun-dried fish, Walter. Blame the menopause, son. No amount of oil is going to restore their youthful beauty and moist elasticity. The bloom has gone. The dew evaporated. Like Mrs Crabtree, give up your dreams. Your time and theirs is over.

WALTER: The wood! The wood! The carvings! My carvings! The pear!

ROBERT: The lime!

WALTER: Yes!

ROBERT: And where do I find this pair of lime carvings, Walter? I didn't know anything about this. Where have you hidden them?

WALTER: I'm not talking to you.

ROBERT: Oh, yes you are, sweetheart. You're talking to me because I am the only one here talking to you and because I find all this deeply interesting. Now where are they?

WALTER: (*Sweetly.*) There aren't any.

ROBERT: Then what are we talking about, you old dodderer? Have we been having a totally meaningless conversation here?

WALTER: I mean I haven't got started yet. I can't make up my mind.

ROBERT: Walter, you have no mind to make up. Your mind disintegrated a thousand years ago under a constant barrage of EST.

WALTER: You know what you are, don't you?

ROBERT: Tell me.

WALTER: You're a prick!

ROBERT: Walter, never a truer word was said. That's exactly what I am, what all we males are; walking, talking, breathing, living pricks. But the point to remember, Walter, is that this particular prick cares for you, you old sod. So much so that I am exceptionally worried about this sudden craze, in one already so crazed anyway, for carving. What are we going to carve, Walter? Voodoo dolls? Dildoes? A complete crucifixion scene? Beware unbridled ambition, Walter, especially at your advanced age of senility.

WALTER: (*Starting to cry.*) Why do you say things to me?

He lifts the floor cloth to his face but ROBERT hurriedly stops him and, fishing in his pocket, brings out a crumpled hankie which he holds out.

ROBERT: No, Walter. Here, use this.

WALTER: (*Ignoring the hankie.*) I've got to clean the floor.

ROBERT: Not until we've stopped discussing things. You see, the reason why I am so worried about you is that, in order to carve wood; be it lime, pear, oak, or ebony, you need tools. And tools for carving have sharp edges, extremely sharp. And someone like yourself, Walter, who has difficulty not wetting his pants, will have even more difficulty in keeping from cutting himself and I have already had one stern lecture today about not helping you go before your time.

WALTER: Go? Go where? Where am I going?

ROBERT: Why, Walter, to whatever great big hallucination in the sky burnt-out schizophrenics go to. So, should I see you with a chisel in your hand, or a Stanley knife, or any other such lethal weapon, I would be forced to remove same for your own protection and before irreparable damage was done. Do I make myself clear?

WALTER: What about a penknife?

ROBERT: A penknife.

WALTER: A penknife.

ROBERT: A penknife you may have... provided it's blunt.

WALTER: Oh, Mr Benham... you're teasing me again.

ROBERT: (*Placing his hands on WALTER's shoulders.*) Oh, Walter, Walter. I've really, for some grotesque reason, some truly inexplicable reason, grown quite fond of you. I'll miss you when you've gone.

WALTER: What if you should go first, Mr Benham?

ROBERT: True. True I hadn't thought of that. Out of the mouths of babes and schizos. And where do you think I'll go to?

WALTER: To whichever great big whatever in the sky stupid young pricks go to. Can I clean my floor now?

ROBERT: Of course you may clean your floor. But not with that. (*He takes the tub of lavatory cleaner.*) I'll get you something else. In the meantime start with that... (*The floor cloth.*)

WALTER nods and, aided by ROBERT, gets down on his knees. ROBERT watches him for a moment and then turns to go just as TRACEY enters pushing a wheelchair. She indicates the occupant.

TRACEY: Rosemary.

ROBERT: Lavender.

TRACEY: What?

ROBERT: Oh, I thought you were conducting a word-association test.

TRACEY: Don't you ever stop?

ROBERT: Not if I can help it and then only to recharge. Can't keep it up all the time you know.

TRACEY: Why is Walter on his knees?

ROBERT: An attack of religion. Like St Paul on the road to Damascus. Just another smitten schizophrenic to mislead poor suffering humanity with his delusions. So... this is Rosemary... Rosemary who we've all been waiting for... the long anticipated Rosemary. How do you do, Rosemary?

He stretches out his hand. She gives no indication of having seen it. To TRACEY.

Well this one's certainly going to be the life and soul of the party. Are you going to invoke the presence of mother superior or am I?

TRACEY: I'll do it.

She pushes the wheelchair to a table and starts to go.

ROBERT: And I will fetch and carry for my friend Walter.

WALTER: Thank you, Mr Benham.

ROBERT: Think nothing of it, Walter. What are friends for but to impose upon? Now don't you go having any revelations while I'm away. Epistles from Saint Walter to the Kensingtonians and Hamsteadites would be about as welcome as a sex shop catalogue in Fortnum and Mason's.

ROBERT and TRACEY have both gone their separate ways.

WALTER stares at ROSEMARY, gets up and crosses slowly to her. He stands beside her wheelchair and then tentatively stretches out a hand and places it on her shoulder. There is a long moment before her eyes move to look at the hand. Then she looks out front again.

ROSEMARY: I shouldn't be here you know.

WALTER: Wh... wh... where should you be then?

ROSEMARY: At home.

WALTER: This is a home.

ROSEMARY: In my own flat. I have this very nice little flat in a friend's house. At least I thought she was a friend. I could stay there because I cleaned for her. Now she's done this to me.

WALTER: Who?

ROSEMARY: Edith. I know it was her.

WALTER: Who's Edith?

ROSEMARY: I told you.

WALTER: Oh. (*He thinks for a moment.*) I knew her.

ROSEMARY: Knew who?

WALTER: Edith.

ROSEMARY frowns in total bewilderment. WALTER, seeing the approach of MATRON and TRACEY, removes his hand and retires. The two women enter and approach the wheelchair.

MATRON: Well well well, so this is Rosemary. (*She stops and looks down at the floor cloth.*) And what is this?

TRACEY: I think it's Walter's.

MATRON: Walter? Do you know anything about this?

WALTER nods. MATRON waits.

(*Finally.*) Well?

WALTER kneels down and resumes his cleaning.

What are you doing? Walter! What's he doing?

16

                    Cleaning the floor!

TRACEY *shrugs*.

                    Well stop him. Stop him! It's not for him to clean
                    the floor. Walter! Get up. Immediately, do you
                    hear?

WALTER: I spilt it. Oil.

MATRON: It doesn't matter. It's still not your place to clean
                    it up. Whatever will Rosemary think of us? Help
                    him to his feet, nurse. Look at you. Your knees
                    are covered in the stuff. And your hands. You're a
                    mess. Take him away. Clean him up.

TRACEY: Yes, matron.

WALTER: But...

MATRON: Don't argue, Walter. Go with nurse.

*MATRON turns back to ROSEMARY. TRACEY starts
to lead WALTER out. He turns back and shouts.*

WALTER: I'm Walter!

MATRON: Thank you, Walter, we know who you are.

WALTER: I was telling Rosemary.

MATRON: That's very nice. I'm sure Rosemary appreciates
                    the gesture.

TRACEY has almost got WALTER out.

WALTER: She's wrong you know.

TRACEY: What?

WALTER: Nobody knows who I am.

They go. MATRON pulls up a chair beside ROSEMARY and sits. She glances at the papers in her hand.

MATRON: Now then... yes... (*She looks up.*) ...Well, Rosemary, welcome to The Grange. We're so happy to have you here with us.

ROSEMARY: (*Turning to her.*) They took me out of my flat you know.

MATRON: Yes... Yes, they did. That's a... well, that's because you can no longer look after yourself...

ROSEMARY: Who says?

MATRON: ...properly.

ROSEMARY: It was Edith, wasn't it? She snitched. Well she made a mistake. Yes, that's it. It's all a big mistake. I want to go back... please.

MATRON: I'm sorry, my dear, I'm afraid that's simply not possible.

ROSEMARY: It's my home.

MATRON: No, this is your home now. And we will try and make it as happy and as comfortable a home for you as we can.

ROSEMARY: What about my things?

MATRON: Your things have been brought here, all you need. When you've been shown to your room and...

ROSEMARY: No, my other things. My chairs and tables, my bed, my bureau, my things.

MATRON: I really am sorry, my dear, but it just isn't possible.

ROSEMARY: What will happen to them?

MATRON: They will all be taken care of. Now...

ROSEMARY: I've left them to people you know, in my will.

MATRON: Yes, I know. I promise you, it's all in hand. A firm of solicitors has been assigned to look after your affairs.

She tries to take ROSEMARY's hand. ROSEMARY gently but firmly resists.

Would you like a cup of tea?

ROSEMARY: (*Starts to laugh, then cry.*) I'm dying and you ask me if I'd like a cup of tea.

MATRON: No, no, don't be silly. You're not dying.

ROSEMARY: Then why else have I been sent here?

MATRON: I told you, so that we can take care of you. The court decided in your own interest...

ROSEMARY: Court? Who asked the court to stick its nose in my affairs?

MATRON: Look, let's not talk about it anymore right now. Why don't I introduce you to some of the others so that you can start making friends right away?

ROSEMARY shakes her head

You're not shy are you? A big girl like you?

ROSEMARY: (*Gives her a withering look and then turns away again.*) I only had a few things you know. Not very much. Hardly anything at all really.

MATRON: (*Brightly.*) Oh, look! There's Mrs Crabtree... and Mr Putnam... and there's Miss Wilkinson.

ROSEMARY: Funny, I can't remember when last I got a birthday card.

MATRON: (*Looking at her papers.*) It's not your birthday.

ROSEMARY: I know it's not my birthday. I was thinking.

MATRON: Don't worry. We'll make sure your birthday is not forgotten. (*Even more brightly.*) Oh, and here's Robert.

ROBERT enters. He is carrying a plastic container.

MATRON: Robert, where are Rosemary's things?

ROBERT: There's a suitcase of sorts in the hall. Would that be it? I'll see to it.

MATRON: (*To ROSEMARY.*) Is there anything you need right now, my dear?

ROSEMARY shakes her head. MATRON gets up.

All right, I'll leave Robert to look after you and we'll have a nice long chat later. (*To ROBERT.*) What's that in your hand?

ROBERT: Detergent.

MATRON: What for?

ROBERT: The floor.

MATRON: Did you tell Walter to clean the floor?

ROBERT: Walter?

MATRON: The very fact that you have to repeat the name means that the answer is "yes."

ROBERT: No, matron. (*Innocently.*) When I came in here he was already at it. But he was going to use lavatory cleaner so I took that from him, told him to stop, and went to fetch this. Was he at it when you came in?

MATRON: Hmn... Well, as there is nobody else available at the moment, would you mind doing it?

ROBERT: Of course not, matron.

MATRON: I found him on his hands and knees. Walter should not be asked to do menial tasks. The man was a chartered accountant.

ROBERT: Such a come-down in the world.

MATRON: We can all of us come down in this world, Mr Benham, and don't you forget it.

ROBERT: Yes, matron.

He watches her go.

No, matron, three bags full, matron. (*Turns to ROSEMARY.*) Well, Rosemary...

ROSEMARY: Miss Davis.

ROBERT: (*Pause.*) I see. (*Pause.*) Well, Miss Rosemary Davis, would you care for some tea?

ROSEMARY: (*The tears start again.*) Now I know I'm dying... TWO cups of tea!

ROBERT: Hey hey hey! (*He does a bit of sparring.*) Taken off guard and unprepared for that sudden uppercut that came out of nowhere, the champion felt his knees buckle. He swayed on rubbery legs before crashing to the canvas... (*He drops to his knees.*) ...floored by that vicious wit.

ROSEMARY starts to laugh. ROBERT lifts an arm and peers around at her from beneath his armpit.

Tea?

ROSEMARY: Yes please... Robert.

BLACKOUT.

SCENE TWO

A few days later.

There is the sound of half a dozen or more old folk singing around an out of tune piano.

CHORUS: We've been together now for forty years, and it don't seem a day too much.
There ain't a lady living in the land, that I'd swop for my dear old Dutch,
No there ain't a lady living in the land, what I'd swop for my dear old Dutch.

LIGHTS UP to reveal ROSEMARY now seated in a chair by a table. Her wheelchair is beside her.

WALTER enters, stops, looks at her, advances until he is close to the table.

WALTER: I'm Walter.

ROSEMARY: Yes, I know. (*She turns to look at him.*)

WALTER: You're Edith.

ROSEMARY: No, I'm Rosemary.

WALTER: Yes, Rosemary.

She looks away again.

Don't you want to sing? Join in the singing? Singing's good for you. It makes you feel good. Good good good. That's why people do it.

ROSEMARY: It's stopped.

WALTER: It will start again. It's Miss Wilkinson playing the piano.

ROSEMARY: Oh.

WALTER: She's very good.

ROSEMARY: Yes.

WALTER: But she needs a rest.

Silence.

ROSEMARY: Great performers, those blessed with a wonderful talent, opera singers for instance, they get paid thousands of pounds to appear, did you know that?

WALTER: I knew that.

ROSEMARY: Film stars.

WALTER: Film stars.

ROSEMARY: Concert artistes.

WALTER: Concerts.

ROSEMARY: Thousands and thousands...

WALTER: Thousands and thousands...

ROSEMARY: Of pounds.

WALTER: Pounds.

Silence.

ROSEMARY: Have you seen them?

WALTER: Oh yes. (*Pause.*) Who?

ROSEMARY: Those two.

WALTER looks around, sees nobody, frowns.

Nurse Williams... and him!

WALTER: Oh.

ROSEMARY: They've been at it again, haven't they? They're always at it.

WALTER: Yes, at it again. Dirty little snipes.

ROSEMARY: It's sin.

WALTER: Sin.

ROSEMARY: And that's the trouble with young people today, they don't believe in sin anymore.

WALTER: No. Don't you want to join in?

ROSEMARY: What!

WALTER: The singing. When it starts again.

ROSEMARY turns away, looks straight ahead again.

Don't you want to make friends?

ROSEMARY: Friends? Friends? Huh! No point in making friends. You can't trust anybody these days.

WALTER: You can trust me.

ROSEMARY: I don't know you.

WALTER: Yes you do. I'm Walter.

The singing starts again.

CHORUS: The boy I love is up in the gallery, the boy I love is looking down at me...

ROBERT enters, joining in the singing as he goes.

ROBERT: There he is, can't you see? A waving of his handkerchief, as merry as the robin that sits in the tree.

WALTER: You've been at it again haven't you? You dirty little bugger.

ROBERT: At it? At what, Walt?

WALTER: At it! It! It! At it!

ROBERT: A tit, a tit, my kingdom for a tit! What exactly is the meaning of your cryptic incantation, Walter? What exactly is this thing called "it"?

WALTER: You know.

ROBERT: Indeed I do.

WALTER: And you've been at it.

ROBERT: Indeed I have. Why else would I be singing as merrily as the robin that sits in the tree? Post coitus tristus, Walter, is for the mare and the woman, leave them to it. And Trace is feeling quite a bit triste right at this moment.

WALTER: You shouldn't do it, Mr Benham. Distressing gentlefolk.

ROBERT: Walter, I had a quick knee-trembler in the broom cupboard. That is what convenient broom cupboards are for. At least it was behind a closed door, consenting adults in private. So what's the complaint?

WALTER: We could still hear you.

ROBERT: Then you shouldn't have been standing there with your head glued to the door. Lucky for you I didn't open it or you would have had more of an ear-bashing than you bargained for. You shouldn't do that, Walter, bringing yourself on at your age. It could cause a heart flutter, un soufflé du coeur. Only, in your case, scrambled would be more apt. People who watch are called voyeurs, what are people who listen called? Auditors? Now that is apt for a perverted chartered accountant. Wouldn't you agree, Rosemary?

ROSEMARY: You say the most dreadful things, kindly do not include me in this conversation.

ROBERT: And as for you, you naughty girl, who didn't eat her lunch then?

ROSEMARY: What's going to happen to you when you die?

ROBERT: If I'm not put in the fridge, the oven, or the earth pretty damn quick I'll stink to high heaven.

ROSEMARY: That's the only part of you that will get to heaven, the stink.

ROBERT: (*Shadow boxing around WALTER.*) Stunned by this vicious left hook, the champion reeled back against the ropes, desperately trying to evade the flurry of blows.

ROSEMARY: Robert what are you trying to do?

ROBERT: Stay alive, Rosemary, stay alive. Maybe not as merrily as the robin...

WALTER: I knew him.

ROBERT: Who, Walter?

WALTER: Robin.

ROBERT: Of course you did... but at least stay alive.

ROSEMARY: Well you're making a pretty lousy job of it.

ROBERT: Am I?

ROSEMARY: It's all show, all pretend. Scaredy cat.

ROBERT: The knock-out punch. The champion is carried dazed and bloodied from the ring.

And he staggers out.

WALTER: It's no good talking to him. You can talk to him till you're blue in the face. It's like talking to the man in the moon. You might as well talk to yourself. Talk to a brick wall. (*Shouting after him.*) I'll report you to matron, that's what I'll do!

> *He turns to look at ROSEMARY but she has withdrawn again.*

>> Well... I suppose I'd best get on then... yes, lots to do... (*Silence*) ...what are you going to do? (*Silence.*) Well, I'd best get on then. (*He looks around and moves over to where the oil was spilled, looks down at the floor.*) I wanted to clean it up but matron wouldn't let me. I would have enjoyed cleaning it up. Would have given me something to do.

ROSEMARY: Yes, I would have enjoyed it too. Only I would have fallen over.

> *WALTER turns to looks at her.*

>> I fall over you see.

WALTER: (*Nodding.*) I see.

ROSEMARY: That's the reason they forced me out of my flat. I kept falling over.

WALTER: But you can walk.

ROSEMARY: Of course I can walk. But I fall over.

WALTER: Going downstairs like.

ROSEMARY: Going up stairs.

WALTER: I used to do that. It was because I'd forget to lift my legs. Mr Benham pointed that out to me. "You're not lifting your legs, Walter," he said.

ROSEMARY: And then I fell against the stove and burnt my arm, quite severely, and that was when nosey Edith called them in and so they forced me out of my flat. I suspect really she wanted me out. I suspect

	she wanted to get rid of me because it was only a minor burn. See? (*She holds up her arm to reveal a gauze bandage held on with tape.*)
WALTER:	No, no, it doesn't look like a minor burn. No no no, it looks very nasty.
ROSEMARY:	What are you talking about? You can't see the burn. That's the bandage. You're looking at the bandage.
WALTER:	It looks a big one.
ROSEMARY:	Of course it's a big one. That's because they have to be ultra-careful, careful infection won't seep in, so they give the edges plenty of cover. They don't want to be sued for negligence now do they? Do you want to see it?

WALTER shakes his head, a most emphatic "No."
ROSEMARY withdraws the arm.

	It doesn't look so bad now. Sort of pink... and brown... and white.
WALTER:	I'll make you a stick, Rosemary. Two sticks. I'll carve them for you. I have this penknife you see. It's very sharp. Mr Benham doesn't know I've got it. I've got other things too he doesn't know about.
ROSEMARY:	For carving.
WALTER:	Yes. It's my hobby you see.
ROSEMARY:	What do you carve?
WALTER:	I haven't carved anything yet. But I will. I'll think of something. I could start with a stick.

ROSEMARY turns away.

Two sticks! One for each hand. Then you can balance more easily. It will be more difficult to fall over. I could be very good at carving.

ROSEMARY: I am told you were a chartered accountant.

WALTER: Was I?

ROSEMARY: That's what I was told.

WALTER: No, I don't think so. You must have misheard. I was a tax inspector.

ROSEMARY: Oh. (*Pause.*) You must have made a lot of enemies.

WALTER: I did get some a... a... a... anomynous letters. Yes. I did.

ROSEMARY: Nasty ones.

WALTER: Oh, dear me, yes. Very nasty. Very nasty indeed. I don't recall ever suffering any personal abuse though in the form of GBH. I may have done, but I don't recall it. Funny people though, taxpayers. You can never tell with them.

ROSEMARY: I... am an actress.

WALTER: (*After thinking about this for a moment.*) Was.

ROSEMARY: What?

WALTER: Was. You were an actress.

ROSEMARY: No no, I am an actress.

WALTER: No no, you were an actress. You're retired now.

ROSEMARY: No no! You don't understand Walter. That's the beauty of our profession, we never retire. We can

	go on playing parts till the day we... die.
WALTER:	Oh, I see. Yes. Were you playing a part before you... before you came here?
ROSEMARY:	I was resting.
WALTER:	I see. Not re-tired, just tired. He he he.
ROSEMARY:	(*Cold.*) That is an expression we use in our profession, resting, meaning I was temporarily unemployed. Of course I was drawing my pension but if someone, a producer say, or a director, had asked for me, I would have been available.
WALTER:	What part were you playing before you were resting?
ROSEMARY:	Miss Wilkinson must be having a long break. They haven't started singing again.
WALTER:	(*Not to be put off.*) What part?
ROSEMARY:	What?
WALTER:	Before you were resting.
ROSEMARY:	Oh, I was on television.
WALTER:	Were you? Maybe I saw you. We watch a lot of television here.
ROSEMARY:	Oh, no, I don't think so.
WALTER:	Yes, maybe I did. Maybe I saw you. What was it you were on?
ROSEMARY:	Well, it was a very small part, like a guest appearance, and it went out very late at night, too late for you to have seen it.

WALTER: Oh.

ROSEMARY: So you couldn't have. Still, you never know, maybe they'll repeat it at a more sensible hour. If they do I'll make sure to tell you in good time.

WALTER: Yes. We could look for it in the TV Times.

ROSEMARY: Yes.

WALTER: Yes. I would like that. I would like to see you on television. I could point to it and say, "Look, I know her." Yes, I'd like that. We watch a lot of television here. And sing. When Miss Wilkinson feels up to playing the piano. Of course she's not as good as she used to be. Her fingers, you know, get a bit stiff. If you ask me it's all those rings she wears, stops the blood. But she has a go. You should join in next time, Rosemary, especially now I know you are in the performing arts. I don't think there's anyone else here who's an actress. You would have been on schedule D then. I might have done your tax returns. (*They both look out front. Silence. Then he turns back to her.*) An actress...well I never. Who would have thought it? I remember... I remember...

ROSEMARY: (*Prompting.*) What?

WALTER: When I was a wee lad, my dad... I think it was my dad, maybe it was someone else... I don't know... he used to take me to the Music Halls you know. Yes, The Hackney Empire it was, sometimes the Dalston Empire. We used to live in that neck of the woods then, when I was a lad. Shoreditch.

ROSEMARY: Oh, Shoreditch. Shoreditch was very famous in Elizabethan times you know.

WALTER: Was it?

ROSEMARY: Oh, yes. Some very famous actors and playwrights and things lived in Shoreditch in those far away times.

WALTER: Did they now? Well I never. Like who for example?

ROSEMARY: Famous ones.

WALTER: Well I never. There were some grand Music Halls too as I remember, in Shoreditch, Whitechapel. All gone now though I shouldn't wonder. Terrible, terrible. Did you ever do the halls?

ROSEMARY: Music Hall! Oh, no! I was strictly legitimate.

WALTER: Legitimate?

ROSEMARY: That's an expression we use meaning straight. You know, straight plays, be they comedy or drama.

WALTER: Never went to plays much, not that I recall. Don't remember seeing any plays. Oh, no, not plays.

ROSEMARY: I want to show you something. Where's my bag? Oh, there it is... (*On the wheelchair.*) ...Would you mind?

WALTER gets the bag and passes it to her. Then he sits in the wheelchair.

That's my wheelchair!

WALTER: (*Rising.*) Oh, sorry, sorry! I'm sorry, Rosemary. (*He takes another seat.*) Sorry.

ROSEMARY has opened the bag and is taking out various odds and ends: a purse, a bunch of keys, well worn grubby buff envelopes that could contain anything official but probably don't, an old-fashioned compact and, finally, a yellowed scrap of newsprint which she passes to him.

ROSEMARY: Take great care. It's fragile.

He takes it, looks, hands it back.

No, no, read it.

WALTER: I can't. Can't see without my glasses.

ROSEMARY: Where are your glasses?

WALTER: I think I left them somewhere.

ROSEMARY: Where? Where?

WALTER: (*Growing agitated.*) I don't remember.

ROSEMARY: When?

WALTER: I don't remember!

ROSEMARY: Think! Think!

WALTER: I am thinking, Rosemary.

ROSEMARY: Hmph! Well you'd better get a new pair then. You'll damage your eyes.

WALTER: Yes. You read it to me.

ROSEMARY: It's from The Daily Mail.

WALTER: What about your glasses?

ROSEMARY glares at him. Does she need glasses to read what is written on her heart?

ROSEMARY: "Look After The Pennies", the new play which

opened last night at The Watergate Theatre... I won't read you all of it, just my bit... It says... "Keep your eye on Miss Rosemary Davis. This young actress, I believe she is just eighteen, who plays the part of the maid, is a young lady who is certain to go places. I will even go so far as to say we have here a future star."

WALTER watches as she starts to put away the contents of the bag.

WALTER: He liked you.

Finally the scrap of paper is returned to the bag and ROSEMARY sniffs loudly. It is a proud sniff.

Well. (*Silence.*) It's a pity you were never on the halls. You could have been another... (*He concentrates very hard.*) ... another Florrie Ford, Marie Lil... lil... Lloyd, Gertie Gitana.

He starts to sing. ROSEMARY stares straight ahead.

Though your heart be full of pain, never mind,
Though your face should lose its smile, never mind,
For there's sunshine after rain,
And gladness follows pain
You'll be happy once again, never mind.

BLACKOUT.

SCENE THREE

CHORUS: Keep right on to the end of the road, Keep right on to the end,
Though the way be hard and the road be long, keep right on to the end.

LIGHTS UP to reveal ROBERT standing looking out of the window which we assume is in the fourth wall. He has earphones on and a Walkman hooked on his belt.

ROSEMARY enters, walking with the aid of two sticks, looks around as though expecting to find someone, walks up to ROBERT.

ROSEMARY: Robert?... Robert!

She prods him with the stick.

ROBERT: Ouch! (*He turns around, raises his eyes heavenwards, takes off the earphones and switches off the Walkman.*) Yes, Rosemary, what can I do for you?

ROSEMARY: Where is Walter?

ROBERT: He's having one of his off days.

ROSEMARY: That was yesterday.

ROBERT: Walter's off day can last two or three, or more.

ROSEMARY: Where is he then?

ROBERT: In his room of course.

ROSEMARY: Oh, that's all right then. Nothing has happened to him.

ROBERT: No, he's fine. Well, he's drugged up to the eyeballs but, when he eventually comes round, he'll be as right as rain.

ROSEMARY: Oh, good.

ROBERT: Acid rain. Can I go back to my music now?

ROSEMARY: What are you listening to? Modern rubbish I expect.

ROBERT: Quite right, Rosemary dear, fairly modern rubbish. Shoshtakovitch, Symphony number eight.

ROSEMARY: Oh, a symphony. That's all right then.

ROBERT: (*As he helps her into a chair.*) I'm so glad you approve. You're quite knowledgeable about symphonic music are you?

ROSEMARY: I like the 1812 Overture. Do you know that one?

ROBERT: Ye-es. That's by Borodin isn't it?

ROSEMARY: No, dear. It's Rachmaninov.

ROBERT: Oh, yes, of course. Pardon me.

ROSEMARY: What did you say that was?

ROBERT: Shostakovich number eight. I was just into the third movement when you so rudely and painfully interrupted my listening pleasure.

ROSEMARY: I'm sorry. I wanted to know what had happened to Walter. I'm relieved to hear he's all right.

ROBERT: And I'm relieved to hear that you're relieved. Perhaps you'd like to hear some of this too... (*He holds out the earphones.*) ...it will make a change from "*She'll Be Coming Round The Mountain*" and "*My Old Man Said Follow The Van.*"

ROSEMARY: Oh, I like that one. (*Singing.*) My old man said follow the van but don't dilly-dally on the way.

ROBERT: Very nice, dear.

ROSEMARY: Walter started to teach me the words but then he found he couldn't remember them. But we were in luck because Beryl Crabtree knew the whole song.

ROBERT: Bully for Beryl. Look, do you want to hear this or don't you? You should be more catholic in your musical tastes.

ROSEMARY: Oh, no! I couldn't be Catholic in anything. My father was a clergyman you know and he never held with high church. Half way to Rome he called it. Is this Catholic music?

ROBERT: You're wandering, Rosemary. Try and keep your mind on the straight and narrow. Catholic is merely an expression meaning wide, all-embracing.

ROSEMARY: It was only a tiny church, very simple, very plain. Even poor, you might say.

ROBERT: Might I?

ROSEMARY: A small parish in Kent. Do you know Kent?

ROBERT: Not intimately, no.

ROSEMARY: It's very beautiful, especially in the Spring, with the apple blossom, and the young lambs gambolling away.

ROBERT: Gambol, gambol, while you may, the abattoir's not far away.

ROSEMARY: It's no good talking about Kent to Walter. He keeps asking if there were any Music Halls. How would I know if there were any Music Halls in Kent? Still, if that's what God wanted of him...

ROBERT: To enquire about Music Halls in Kent?

ROSEMARY: No! Daddy! His lot in life was to tend a small flock in a tiny parish church in a corner of England. It's like the children's hymn says... (*Singing.*) You in your small corner and I in mine. (*Pause.*) I miss him so much.

ROBERT: Who?

ROSEMARY: Daddy. When he died I was only thirteen.

ROBERT: Unlucky for some.

ROSEMARY: He was such a nice man, such a good man, so gentle, so kind.

ROBERT: And you still miss him.

ROSEMARY: Oh, yes, even after all these years. Why did he have to die so young?

ROBERT: Maybe he was one of the proverbial sort who have a tendency towards that kind of thing.

ROSEMARY: You're very smart aren't you, Robert?

ROBERT: Am I? How nice of you to say so, Rosemary. That's the nicest compliment I've been paid today.

ROSEMARY: It wasn't meant as a compliment, you silly goose. It was meant to be sarcastic, or ironic, I can never remember which is which. Anyway, it was meant to be a cutting remark. I don't like to be cruel. Cruelty is not a part of my nature. But there are times when it is a case of spare the rod and spoil the child and you need to be reminded that we are all human and we all have feelings.

ROBERT: I am duly chastised.

ROSEMARY: Look at Walter.

ROBERT: Pardon me, Rosemary, but sometimes I'd rather not.

ROSEMARY: He has been hurt... by life... life has hurt him badly. I understand that.

ROBERT: Yes, I suppose you do. Were you ever given a fair chance, Rosemary?

ROSEMARY: Nurse Williams has feelings too.

ROBERT: What suddenly brought her into the conversation?

ROSEMARY: The way you behave with her. Worse, the things you say...

ROBERT: Uh-uh! (*He raises an admonishing finger.*) Now, Rosemary dear, you're stepping on eggshells here. Other people's relationships are no concern of yours.

ROSEMARY: I was only going to say...

ROBERT: Uh-uh!

ROSEMARY: No, of course you don't want to hear it, do you? Because you know how wrong your behaviour is.

ROBERT: Rosemary, another word and I am going to have to chastise you. Now put these on and shut up.

ROSEMARY: (*Holding the earphones.*) What did you say his name was?

ROBERT: Who?

ROSEMARY: This composer.

ROBERT: Shostakovich.

ROSEMARY: Is he Jewish?

ROBERT: What?

ROSEMARY: Jewish... Is he Jewish?

ROBERT: I really don't know. Why should he be Jewish?

ROSEMARY: His name ends in a vitch. Most people I've met whose name ends in a vitch are Jewish.

ROBERT: He's Russian. Was Russian.

ROSEMARY: Oh, well, that explains it then. Yes, he's probably Jewish. If he's Russian or Polish and his name ends in a vitch he's most likely Jewish.

ROBERT: Does it make any difference to anything, Rosemary?

ROSEMARY: No, I was just curious. Curiosity...

ROBERT: Killed the cat.

ROSEMARY: ...is part of my training. I am an actress you know.

ROBERT: Yes, I know. Everyone in the Grange knows. Walter has done nothing else for a week but spread the news of your thespian pretensions. He's told the butcher, the baker, and the candlestick maker every time they've made a delivery, and they've gone off and told everyone they know. Your fame is spreading like a bushfire.

ROSEMARY withdraws.

What's the matter? (*Silence.*) Did I say something? Have I hurt your feelings? (*Silence.*) What did I say?

ROSEMARY pulls herself up straight and sniffs loudly.

Jesus!

ROSEMARY: I'll thank you not to blaspheme in my presence, Mr Benham. Kindly refrain from taking the name of our Lord in vain. I know these days it's considered a smart thing to do...

ROBERT: Bullshit.

ROSEMARY: (*Another loud sniff.*) You are so course, Robert.

ROBERT: Okay, from now on I'll stick to Gordon Bennett, all right? (*No response.*) Hey, Missus, look at me. I'm talking to you. See these? They're lips. They're moving. (*No response.*) Gordon Bennett!

ROSEMARY: Who's Gordon Bennett?

ROBERT: I haven't the faintest idea, Rosemary, who effing Gordon Bennett is. And don't ask me if he's Jewish because I've no idea about that either. Neither do I know if he's a Catholic.

ROSEMARY: There is no need to raise your voice. It is unbecoming in an educated man.

ROBERT: Who says I'm educated?

ROSEMARY: Oh, come off it, you silly person. Anybody with half an eye can see you're educated. Well just listen to you, the way you talk. It's an absolute giveaway.

ROBERT: Really. Well I do have a couple of university degrees if that's any criterion.

ROSEMARY: What are you doing then, working here?

ROBERT: That has nothing to do with you, Miss Rosemary

Davis.

ROSEMARY: University degrees! There you are then.

ROBERT: No, Rosemary, there I am not. I've got a friend, he was my room-mate in college, he's got an honours in history and he's on the buses.

ROSEMARY: Why?

ROBERT: My my my, we are an inquisitive little busybody today. Because he likes driving a bus. Satisfied? He likes stopping at red lights. It gives him time to think. As far as the world is concerned at the moment, my degrees don't add up to a pig's fart in a brass band.

ROSEMARY: You're terrible!

ROBERT: Why are you laughing then?

ROSEMARY: Pigs don't fart in brass bands.

She collapses in a fit of mirth. ROBERT enjoys it too. They eventually recover.

ROBERT: That's the first time I've heard you laugh, really laugh.

ROSEMARY: To be quite honest, Robert, there hasn't been much in my life to laugh about. I tried. I really tried. (*She takes his hand.*) I had such dreams, Robert. Oh, I had such dreams.

ROBERT: Yes. I know. I know.

ROSEMARY: But everything seemed to just fall apart. Nothing ever seemed to go right for me. And I had no one to turn to, no one to help.

ROBERT: Hey, you old charmer, we're being watched. (*He indicates off-stage.*) If we're not careful, people will start to talk.

ROSEMARY: Oh, Robert! (*She gives him an affectionate push and picks up the earphones.*) I'll listen to the music now.

ROBERT: (*Taking them back.*) No, no, this is not for you. I don't think you'd really like it.

ROSEMARY: But you wanted me to hear it.

ROBERT: Well I've thought about it and... no... I'll find you something else, something you'll really like.

ROSEMARY: All right, I'll let you choose. Just make sure there isn't a pig in it.

Partly at her own audacity and partly at the image she breaks into another peal of laughter just as MATRON enters.

MATRON: What on earth is all this noise?

ROBERT: (*Looking around.*) Noise?

MATRON: Robert, this habit you have of repeating or questioning everything I say is extremely irritating to say the least.

ROSEMARY: Robert and I were enjoying a little joke, matron.

MATRON: Oh, that's nice. Well it must have been a jolly good one by the sound of it. Tell it to me.

ROSEMARY and ROBERT look at each other and then at MATRON. ROSEMARY turns back to ROBERT to get them out of it.

ROBERT: Well, you see, matron, there was this Irishman, a Scotsman, and a Welshman...

MATRON: Racist jokes are expressly forbidden, Robert, and you know it. We have representatives of all three nations resident in this establishment and their sensibilities will not be abused under any circumstances.

ROBERT: Sorry, matron.

WALTER appears.

MATRON: And look what your racket has done. You've woken Walter. Oh, my God, and he's forgotten his teeth!

TRACEY appears.

Nurse Williams, please take Walter away and put his teeth in. Give him a wash and put his teeth in. He's only half awake.

ROBERT: Or half asleep.

TRACEY leads WALTER away. MATRON sees the walking sticks.

MATRON: What are these?

ROSEMARY: My walking sticks.

MATRON: I haven't seen these before. (*She indicates for one to be handed to her. ROBERT passes it over for examination.*) No rubber tip, no regulation handle. These are not ours. Where did they come from?

ROSEMARY: Walter gave them to me.

MATRON: Walter? Where did he get them from?

ROSEMARY: He made them.

MATRON: Made them? Ridiculous! (*To ROBERT.*) Do you know anything about this?

ROSEMARY: He made them for me. They were a present.

MATRON: Robert, get rid of these please, and get Miss Davis a walking frame.

She starts to go, handing ROBERT the stick as she does so.

ROBERT: But, matron...

She turns back.

Is it really necessary?

MATRON: You're questioning my orders again?

ROBERT: No, matron. It's just that Rosemary seems to manage pretty well with these and... well... a walker... it's so clinical.

MATRON: The safety and well-being of the residents is ultimately my responsibility. There are rules. There are regulations. Now do as I say please, Robert.

She goes. ROBERT turns back to ROSEMARY who is staring straight ahead.

ROBERT: I'm sorry, Rosemary.

ROSEMARY: It really doesn't matter. What difference does it make anyhow?

ROBERT goes out, taking the sticks with him. For a moment ROSEMARY sits staring straight ahead, then she turns and looks in the direction of the departed

MATRON and blows a loud raspberry.

BLACKOUT.

SCENE FOUR

CHORUS: There's a long long trail a winding, into the land of my dreams...

There is the SOUND of an AMBULANCE SIREN and then LIGHTS UP on an empty stage.

ROSEMARY and WALTER enter. He supports her by holding an elbow. They stand for a moment like two lost souls looking out of the window.

ROSEMARY: What do you suppose is happening?

WALTER: They're taking her away, in the ambulance.

ROSEMARY: Yes, I know that. But what do you suppose is happening?

WALTER: They're probably giving her oxygen.

ROSEMARY: Oxygen?

WALTER: They always give you oxygen in an emergency. That's the right thing to do. They do it in aeroplanes too. Without oxygen you can't breathe you see.

ROSEMARY: That's not right.

WALTER: That's what I'm saying.

ROSEMARY: No, no, I don't like to contradict, Walter, but oxygen is what you breathe.

WALTER: But if you're not breathing any then they have to

give it to you.

ROSEMARY thinks about this.

ROSEMARY: But, if she's not breathing, then she must be dead. So what would be the point of giving her oxygen?

WALTER: To start her breathing again, don't you see?

ROSEMARY: How can she start breathing again if she's dead?

WALTER: It's like the kiss of life.

ROSEMARY: Oh, I see. (*Pause.*) What's like the kiss of life?

WALTER: Giving her oxygen.

ROSEMARY: Oh.

The SIREN starts again as the ambulance moves away.

Poor Beryl, I saw it happen you know. I was sitting quite close. One minute there she was, singing away... she had a lovely voice, she could easily have been a singer... and the next second... I think I'd better sit down, Walter, I feel a little shaky.

WALTER: Yes, I think you'd better sit down. (*He helps her into a chair.*) But don't... don't you fall down now.

ROSEMARY: It's a pity it had to happen before lunch. She's missed lunch.

WALTER: She can have lunch at the hospital, if she's up to it.

ROSEMARY: Oh, I don't think she'll be up to it. No, she's missed out on that I'm afraid.

WALTER: Yes, missed out she has. It's fruit compost today.

ROSEMARY: Compote, Walter, fruit compote.

WALTER: That's what I said.

ROSEMARY: I hate it.

WALTER: What?

ROSEMARY: Fruit compote. It always looks like a dog's breakfast. In fact, if you will pardon me saying it, Walter, it looks like the dog's had his breakfast and couldn't keep it down. Poor Mrs Crabtree, Beryl, I do hope she will be all right.

WALTER: Lucky it wasn't Miss Wilkinson or we'd have nobody to play the piano.

ROSEMARY: Oh, Walter! How can you even think of practical matters at a time like this? Typical man.

WALTER expands at what he assumes to be a compliment.

It's very upsetting, something like that happening, right in front of your eyes. She looked terrible, absolutely awful. White as a sheet, and so drawn, and sort of... rattling. What do you suppose it is? Her heart?

WALTER: Could be her heart. Could be something else.

ROSEMARY: Yes. Maybe her kidneys.

WALTER: Kidneys, yes.

ROSEMARY: She's been complaining of back pains. Back pains can mean kidneys. I had a cat died of kidneys. Cats seem to do that.

WALTER: Did it have a bad back?

ROSEMARY: I don't know that, Walter. You do ask some silly questions. Only a vet would know the answer to that. Cats can't talk, tell you what's wrong with them, where they hurt. You can talk to a cat. And, do you know, they understand every word you say? They do. They really do. Every word.

WALTER: Better than people.

ROSEMARY: Oh, much better. Much better than people. People don't listen. They pretend to. They pretend to understand what you're trying to tell them. But they don't really. They're too busy with themselves.

WALTER: And dogs. Dogs too.

ROSEMARY: I'm not so sure about dogs. I don't think I really like dogs all that much. Dirty messy creatures. Cats are so clean, always washing themselves, covering up their business.

WALTER: Their what?

ROSEMARY: Their little jobs.

WALTER: Oh, yes, very clean cats are, very clean. What was your cat called? The one with the kidneys, what was its name?

ROSEMARY: Muffin.

WALTER: Muffin? Muffin? Funny name for a cat. What did you call it that for?

Silence. WALTER moves away and looks out of the window.

WALTER: Muffin! Muffin! Muffin Muffin Muffin... Muffin... funny name for a cat.

ROSEMARY: We used to have muffins for tea.

WALTER: Muffins for tea.

ROSEMARY: In the Rectory. We had a nursery, my sister and me... I... right at the very top of the house. And we had toasted muffins for tea.

WALTER: With jam.

ROSEMARY: Homemade strawberry.

WALTER: So why didn't you call your cat "Strawberry?"

WALTER laughs but ROSEMARY is not amused. The laughter stops.

I bet she was pretty, your sister. I bet I would have liked her. What was her name?

ROSEMARY: Emily. Daddy was fond of the Brontes. Maybe because we lived in a Rectory. She hated me.

WALTER: Oh, no, Rosemary! No no no. I won't have that.

ROSEMARY: She did. She hated me. All her life. When I was little she broke my music box. Quite deliberately. Threw it on the floor, smashed it to pieces under her foot. She said the tune was driving her mad. But it was spite really. She only did it because she hated me.

WALTER: Nobody could hate you, Rosemary.

ROSEMARY: Emily did.

WALTER: I hate her.

ROSEMARY: But she's dead now so let's speak no evil. Do you

	think Beryl is going to die?
WALTER:	She could be dead already.
ROSEMARY:	Oh, Walter, don't even think that!
WALTER:	The roses are dying.
ROSEMARY:	Yes. Winter's coming. I hate winter. The days are so dark, so short.
WALTER:	There's still a few left though. Yellow ones. I like the yellow ones. They last longer. I'd pick you some. But it's not allowed. Regulations you see. Yellow ones last best.
ROSEMARY:	Nothing lasts. (*Pause.*) I'm frightened, Walter.

He goes to sit beside her and takes her hand.

WALTER:	Don't be frightened. It's because of Mrs Crabtree, isn't it? Don't be frightened. There's nothing to be frightened of. I know. I've been there.
ROSEMARY:	Where?
WALTER:	There.
ROSEMARY:	(*Stares at him incredulously.*) Oh, Walter, you do say the strangest things.
WALTER:	There's nothing to be frightened of. I know. (*He taps the side of his head.*) I've been there.

MATRON enters, followed by ROBERT.

ROSEMARY:	Matron?
MATRON:	What is it, Rosemary? I'm busy.

ROSEMARY: I was just wondering, about Beryl, will she be all right?

MATRON exchanges a glance with ROBERT.

MATRON: I'm afraid her condition is quite serious.

WALTER: Will she come back?

MATRON: She's very ill, Walter, I don't think you'll be seeing her again. She'll probably be in hospital for quite some time. (*She turns to go but turns back again.*) And, Rosemary, what is this I hear about you refusing to use your walker?

ROSEMARY: I don't need it.

MATRON: Oh, yes you do. You've already fallen over twice.

ROSEMARY: If I'd had my sticks, the ones Walter gave me, I wouldn't have fallen over, would I?

MATRON: Don't be stubborn, Rosemary.

ROSEMARY: Anyway, Walter helps me. I've got Walter.

MATRON: Don't be a silly girl. Walter can't be at your side all the time. He can't take you to the loo...

ROSEMARY: Matron!

MATRON: ...or put you to bed. Where's her frame, Robert?

ROBERT jerks a thumb over his shoulder.

Fetch it.

ROBERT goes.

ROSEMARY: I won't use it.

MATRON: Do you want to land up in hospital as well? Now do be sensible. Walter, go and find nurse Williams.

WALTER: Where is she?

MATRON: I don't know where she is. If I knew where she was I wouldn't ask you to go and find her.

WALTER: How do I find her if I don't know where she is?

MATRON: Walter!

ROBERT returns with the walker and puts it down fairly close to ROSEMARY.

WALTER: (*Pointing.*) Send him.

MATRON: I asked you to go.

WALTER: Well which way shall I go? Shall I go that way? Or that way? Or...

MATRON: I - don't - care - just - go - and - find - nurse - Williams!

WALTER casts a despairing glance at ROSEMARY. She returns his look but there is obviously nothing they can do. He turns and goes.

MATRON: (*To ROBERT.*) Try and persuade her to use it.

MATRON goes.

ROSEMARY: I won't you know.

ROBERT takes a copy of The Guardian from his jacket pocket and becomes engrossed in it.

What are you reading, Robert?

ROBERT: The newspaper, Rosemary.

ROSEMARY: Oh, very funny, clever clogs.

ROBERT: Well, if you really want to know, I'm looking for another job.

ROSEMARY: (*Stunned.*) Why?

ROBERT: Because I've had a bellyful of stubborn old donkeys, that's why.

ROSEMARY: Meaning me.

ROBERT: Among others.

ROSEMARY: That's not fair. Just because I refuse to use that hideous contraption. I hate it. It makes me feel old.

ROBERT: You are old, Rosemary.

ROSEMARY: Not that old! (*She watches him for a while and then.*) Are you really going to leave us?

ROBERT: If I get another job I would say that is pretty inevitable, wouldn't you?

ROSEMARY: I would be sorry if you went.

ROBERT: Would you?

ROSEMARY: Especially if it was me who was driving you away.

ROBERT: Oh, I don't think you'd be driving me away, Rosemary. I think a taxi would most likely be the order of the day. (*Seeing her face.*) Look, I've just decided to try and get another job in keeping with my academic status. Or improve my academic status. I'm over-qualified already, according to quite a number of rejected applications, I can't do any more damage. The Open University is advertising research scholarships, tell me what you think.

He starts to read. As he does so, ROSEMARY begins to fidget. The fidgeting gets worse until, finally, she struggles to her feet and makes an unsteady course for the walker, grabbing it just in time.

ROBERT: Disability studies - The Disability Studies Group aims to encourage, support, facilitate and co-ordinate interdisciplinary research into all aspects of problems relating to the full participation of disabled people in social living... Or how about this one?... Family research - The Family Research Group encourages research...that's logical... from a multi-disciplinary perspective... Jesus Christ! I mean, Gordon Bennett! What's THAT supposed to mean?...into family belief systems... Systems? Oh, well, plough on... family therapy, development of identity including gender identity... pink bootees and blue bootees are obviously old hat... stress and stability in relationships, social and cultural influences on gender and work conditions... Or what about this one The Human Cognition Research Laboratory...

ROSEMARY: (*At the walker.*) I feel like a caged animal behind this thing.

ROBERT: That's currently engaged in a variety of Artificial Intelligence and Cognitive Science Research Activities, including knowledge acquisition and elicitation, human-computer interfaces, automatic programme understanding and debugging, parallel distribution memory models of natural language parsing...

ROSEMARY: Shit!

ROBERT: My sentiments exactly.

ROSEMARY: I've got to go! I've got to go!

                  BLACKOUT.

ACT TWO
SCENE ONE

The room is in darkness. No more than a glow perhaps from outside the doors.

There is the sound of giggles, shushes, murmurings, a shriek, then...

ROBERT: Gordon Bennett! Will you stop making so much noise. You'll bring matron down around our ears.

TRACEY: Well I'm sensitive just there. If you WILL DO that then... (*Another shriek.*)

ROBERT: Shhhh!... Ow! Watch what you're doing with that heel.

TRACEY: Sorry.

ROBERT: Take them off. Ow!

TRACEY: Sorry... there... better?

ROBERT: Hmn... Ouch!

TRACEY: Now what's the matter?

ROBERT: You nearly poked my eye out, that's what's the matter now.

TRACEY: Sorry.

ROBERT: You will be.

Another shriek from TRACEY.

Shhh...

TRACEY: Stop that, Robert... Stop it!... Robert! You're making me hysterical. Robert!

The light is switched on.

TRACEY, who has been on ROBERT's lap, leaps off and away from the chair, hastily trying to straighten her clothing.

ROBERT turns to see it is WALTER standing there. He is in pyjamas and slippers. TRACEY and ROBERT are in warm, outdoor clothes. ROBERT slips a hand beneath his overcoat to surreptitiously make himself decent.

ROBERT: Bloody hell, Walter! What are you playing at? You could have been the cause of a serious injury.

WALTER: You're at it again aren't you? You're at it.

ROBERT: Not any more we're not. Not now you've gone and put the mockers on it.

WALTER: I don't know... like animals... that's what you're like... like animals.

ROBERT: That's because we are animals, Walter.

WALTER: Animals wouldn't carry on the way you do.

ROBERT: Oh, God! I can't stand it.

TRACEY: Neither can I. I'm going to bed.

She has had time to recover from her fright and is slipping on her shoes.

ROBERT: Why don't we go out again?

TRACEY: At three in the morning? And me up early? You've got to be joking. Anyway, where would we go?

ROBERT: We have an infinite number of choices, your broom cupboard or the back seat of my car. Walter, why are you standing there? Go back to bed like a good boy.

TRACEY: Well that's where I'm going anyway.

ROBERT: (*To WALTER.*) Now see what you've gone and done? I don't know, Walter, sometimes you're neither use nor ornament and that's a fact. (*To TRACEY.*) Take him with you.

TRACEY: Come on, Walter, back to bed.

WALTER: (*Resisting.*) I'm not going.

ROBERT: Don't be a stubborn old bugger, Walter. Go with nurse Williams before I get cross.

WALTER: No! Where's Rosemary? I was looking for Rosemary.

ROBERT: What! At three o'clock in the morning? There's the pot calling the kettle black. Well, you know where her room is, if you've got the energy go to it, old son, and good luck to you. Just make sure you don't wake any of the others. Matron's a dyed in the wool party pooper.

TRACEY: Come on, Walter, don't you listen to him. You really should be in bed you know. You haven't wet it again have you? (*She feels his pyjama leg.*) No.

WALTER: Filth! Filth! No respect! No respect at all have you? You've no respect.

TRACEY: I was only making sure you hadn't...

WALTER: Not you! Him! Mr Benham! It's him I'm talking about. No respect at all.

ROBERT: You're not going to cry are you, Walter? If you're going to start crying I'm going to stop speaking to you.

TRACEY: (*Tugging at his arm.*) Come along, Walter, please! I need my sleep even if you don't.

WALTER: (*Pulling away.*) Nooo... I don't want to. I'm not tired. I won't sleep.

ROBERT: Try a bit of the old top sheet tapping, Walt. That'll send you off, faster than counting sheep.

WALTER: Can't I stay and talk to you, Mr Benham?

ROBERT: (*Who has been going through his pockets.*) No, Walter, I'll be off to bed too. You got any cigarettes, Trace?

TRACEY: No, we smoked them all at the party.

ROBERT: Just as well. My mouth tastes like a Japanese wrestler's jockstrap anyway.

WALTER: No respect.

ROBERT: On the contrary, Walter, I have every respect for Japanese wrestlers. One of those babies sits on your face you'll know he's been there. And he won't be doing it to say he loves you.

TRACEY: He's been like this all evening, Walter, take no notice of him.

WALTER: Oh, I don't. Don't take no notice whatsoever.

ROBERT: Quite right, Walter. Nobody else takes any notice of me anyway, why should you? (*To TRACEY.*) I've told him to go to bed, he's still standing there. Look at him!

TRACEY: I don't want to look at him, thank you. He's all yours. Good night.

She goes.

ROBERT: (*After her.*) Thanks for a great evening! Well, Walter, seems like everybody's deserted us. Just you and me left in the wee small hours. So, my sleep-walking beauty, what did you want to talk about?

WALTER: I don't know.

ROBERT: Good start, good start. I do like conversations that have a definite purpose in mind. I don't suppose you've got a fag have you, Walter?

WALTER: (*Shaking his head.*) I don't smoke, Mr Benham, you know that. I used to. Used to smoke once. Mostly during the war. Are you drunk, Mr Benham?

ROBERT: Drunk? Me? Whatever gave you that idea?

WALTER: I just thought.

ROBERT: Don't think, Walter. You're in the privileged position of not having to. No, I have been to a party... we have been to a party... nurse Williams and I have been to a party. But, in answer to your question, no, I am not drunk, Walter. I am not drunk because I had to drive back here and, having considerable respect for the minions of the law, a rare virtue in this day and age, and for human life and limb, particularly my own, I do not drink and drive.

WALTER: I used to go to parties.

ROBERT: Mostly during the war.

WALTER: Yes. Other times too.

ROBERT: Did you get drunk, Walter?

WALTER: I suppose so. Suppose I must have. I don't remember. But I used to go to parties. I remember that.

ROBERT: You used to smoke, you used to go to parties, you used to get drunk. What gives with you, man? Everything you say is in the past tense. Live for the now, old son. Live for the future. What are you going to do with your life? That's what you must ask yourself. That's what my father always used to go on about to me. So I went to university and got myself two degrees and what am I going to do with my life, Walter? By the looks of it, sweet sod all.

WALTER: You're doing something with your life, Mr Benham.

ROBERT: Am I?

WALTER: You're looking after us old folk. That's nice. And it's nice when people like you.

ROBERT: I don't think anybody likes me much, Walter.

WALTER: I like you, Mr Benham.

ROBERT: Walter, what is this? A proposal of marriage?

WALTER: Don't be silly, Mr Benham. I can't propose to you. You're a man!

ROBERT: Well that solves the gender identification problem.

WALTER: I used to have one of those.

ROBERT: What?

WALTER: What you just said.

ROBERT: Oh.

WALTER: But I'm cured now.

ROBERT: I'm glad.

WALTER: Yes.

ROBERT: Well I'm sorry in a way you're not proposing to me, Walter. But I'd have to turn you down anyway because... well, how can I put this? To be brutally blunt and quite honest with you, I don't really go for the older man.

WALTER: You're teasing me again, Mr Benham.

ROBERT: There, I knew whichever way I put it, I'd hurt your feelings. All I can say is I'm desperately sorry. If it's any consolation to you, after a great deal of consideration, I have decided never to marry anyway.

WALTER: You can't say that.

ROBERT: What do you mean I can't say that? I've just said it.

WALTER: Oh, no. Oh, no. No no no no. You can't say that. No, I won't have that.

ROBERT: Walter, do you know what the shindig, the barbaric ritual tonight was all in aid of?

WALTER shakes his head.

It was to celebrate an engagement. You know, two young people on the threshold of life, their hot little genes boiling over like saucepans of minestrone screaming for immortality. "Get together! Get together! Procreate!" And do you know what happened? They had the biggest flaming flare-up since the great fire of London. He ended up zonked out of his mind and having nine kinds of shit beaten out of him by her brother and she ended up in floods of tears and prostrate with nervous exhaustion. A good start wouldn't you say?

WALTER: I was married. I mean, I am married.

ROBERT: No, Walter, no need to correct yourself. You were married.

WALTER: No, no, I am married.

ROBERT: Were married.

WALTER: I'm still married, you stupid git! She sheshhhh she won't divorce me. It's against her religion you see. Won't give me a divorce. No. And my... my sons... I haven't... She won't divorce me you see.

ROBERT: Walter, your wife died more than three years ago.

WALTER: Never!

ROBERT: Yes.

WALTER: She couldn't have. They would have informed me. I would have been informed. Authorities.

ROBERT: I think you were informed, Walter. You've forgotten, that's all.

WALTER: You're not teasing me, Mr Benham?

ROBERT: Gordon Bennett, Walter! Would I tease you about something like that?

He sees WALTER's trembling hands and takes them in his own. WALTER is crying silently.

Come on, Walter... don't take on... I didn't realise... (*He looks at WALTER's hands.*) ...Walter? What have you done to your fingers?

WALTER: (*Trying to withdraw.*) What? What? Nothing! Nothing! Haven't done anything to them!

ROBERT: Then why are you wearing two plasters? Have you been carving?

WALTER: No!

ROBERT: Expressly against my orders?

WALTER: No!

ROBERT: You're lying, Walter.

WALTER: Scout's honour, Mr Benham.

ROBERT: When an ex-tax inspector says scout's honour then I know he's lying.

WALTER: No!

ROBERT: Then how did you cut your fingers?

WALTER: I never did.

ROBERT: (*Holding up the hands.*) Two plasters.

WALTER: Pricked! I pricked them. They're pricked! Scratched! Pricked!

ROBERT: And just how did you - prick - your - fingers?

WALTER: Roses.

ROBERT: Roses.

WALTER: For Rosemary.

ROBERT: Roses for Rosemary.

WALTER: Yellow ones. They last longer.

ROBERT: Ho-ho-ho! So I was right then. You're a crafty old devil, Walter, aren't you? There's more to you than meets the eye and that's a fact. So, are you going to make an honest woman of her then?

WALTER: What?

ROBERT: Well you're free now, Walter, free as a bird.

WALTER: In that case can I go to bed now, Mr Benham? I'm tired.

ROBERT: So what better way to celebrate your freedom than to fly right into the trap again? Oscar Wilde was right.

WALTER: Was he, Mr Benham? How do you make that out?

ROBERT: Well, he said, a man should get married either when he knows nothing or when he knows everything. Now I know a little more than nothing so I am not going to get married. You, on the other hand, know everything about everything so you should get married. How about it? Get down on your knees and propose to her. Make her the happiest of women.

WALTER: You're a rum cove, Mr Benham, and no mistake.

ROBERT: Now I know you're out of the ark. I thought that expression died out with Charles Dickens.

WALTER: Who?

ROBERT: Charles Dickens.

WALTER: I knew him.

ROBERT: Did you, Walter?

WALTER: Yes. Used to live in Albemarle Terrace. Kept greyhounds.

ROBERT: That's the chap.

WALTER: Funny bloke he was. Went off his head. Don't know what happened to him. Oh, yes... he died you said. Shame.

ROBERT: Come on, Walter, I'll walk you to your door.

They go out. ROBERT switches off the light.

BLACKOUT.

SCENE TWO

CHORUS: There was I, waiting at the church, waiting at the church, waiting at the church, when I found he'd left me in the lurch, Lor! How it did upset me...

LIGHTS UP to reveal ROSEMARY sitting at a table, in front of her a jigsaw puzzle.

MATRON enters.

MATRON: How are you getting on with your jigsaw, Rosemary?

ROSEMARY ignores her. MATRON goes up to the table to take a look.

ROSEMARY: I'm getting on very nicely thank you... on my own.

MATRON reacts to the put-down, surveys the pieces of puzzle, picks one up.

MATRON: Oh, look, this one's easy. It goes in there... (*She places it.*) ...see?

ROSEMARY is furious. MATRON smiles and moves away. ROSEMARY lifts the piece from the puzzle and jumbles it up with others on the side so that she can't find it again.

ROSEMARY: (*Mumbling.*) Some people should learn to mind their own business.

MATRON: (*Turning back.*) What was that, Rosemary?

ROSEMARY: Nothing.

MATRON: Some people are in the position of having to mind other people's business because that is their job. Some people mind other people's business because they care for them. And they go on doing it even when it's not appreciated. So some people should learn not to sulk. Isn't it time you stopped sulking?

ROSEMARY: Who said I was sulking?

MATRON: I say you're sulking.

ROSEMARY: Oh, look! This is an easy piece. It goes in there... See?

MATRON: You should consider yourself extremely lucky.

ROSEMARY: Should I indeed?

MATRON: Indeed you should. You have a nice warm comfortable home, three meals a day, companionship, people to wait on you hand and foot. There are millions of unfortunates in this world who would gladly change places with you, Miss Rosemary Davis, so be grateful for what you have. And you're getting a new room-mate soon, to take Mrs Crabtree's place, so that will be more company for you, won't it?

ROSEMARY: And this is such an easy piece. It goes in there... See?

MATRON: Rosemary, did you hear what I said?

ROSEMARY: I thought Beryl would be coming back.

MATRON: You've known all along she wouldn't be coming back.

ROSEMARY: Has her condition not improved then?

Silence. ROSEMARY searches for another piece, picks one up, starts looking for its place. MATRON returns to sit beside her.

MATRON: Rosemary...

ROSEMARY: (*Starts to cry.*) Excuse me... Where's my bag?

MATRON looks around, sees the bag, passes it to her.

MATRON: Here.

ROSEMARY takes a large handkerchief from the bag. As she does so a piece of paper flutters to the floor. She blows her nose, wipes it, sniffs, picks up another piece of puzzle.

    I hope you will be sociable and make the newcomer feel at home. I mean to say, you are one of the old hands now, aren't you? You know the ropes. So you can help her settle down. It's always strange at first.

ROSEMARY: (*Sniff.*) When's she coming?

MATRON: Just after Christmas. She's spending Christmas with her family.

ROSEMARY: Oh, they're giving her that then. They're giving her Christmas before they get rid of her. Very nice of them.

MATRON: There's just no talking to you when you're in this kind of a mood.

ROSEMARY puts the handkerchief away and picks up another piece of puzzle.

ROSEMARY: Where's Walter?

MATRON: Yes, maybe I'd better find him and get him to talk to you. He seems to be the only one you listen to.

ROSEMARY: Yes, because he talks to me.

MATRON: I talk to you, Rosemary.

ROSEMARY: No you don't. You talk at me. You talk down to me. You talk around me. But you do not talk to me. We've never had a proper talk, about anything.

MATRON: You must realise I am a very busy person with a great deal of responsibility.

ROSEMARY: I know that.

MATRON: I don't have much time for idle chit-chat.

ROSEMARY: Who said anything about idle chit-chat? I didn't say anything about idle chit-chat. I was talking about people talking to people instead of talking at them, that's what I was talking about. Who knows? They might even talk back. Found it!

MATRON: What?

ROSEMARY: That naughty piece that fits in there. I've been worried about that piece for ages.

MATRON gets up and moves away. She is genuinely worried by the criticism. ROSEMARY casts her a quick glance.

            We were going to have a nice long chat the first day I came but we've never had it. "We'll have a nice long chat later," is what you said. Well I'm still waiting. Wait till the cows come home. You were going to tell me about my things. What's happening with my things?

MATRON: Everything has been taken care of.

ROSEMARY: I'm glad to hear it. But they are my things and I would very much like to know just how everything's been taken care of. I mean, has it been taken care of in the same way as my sticks were taken care of? Is that what you call taking care of? My sticks that Walter made for me? That Walter gave me?

MATRON: All right, Rosemary, if you want your walking sticks

	back you may have them. That is, if...
ROSEMARY:	If?
MATRON:	I'll ask Robert what he did with them.
ROSEMARY:	And what if he burnt them? Threw them on the garden fire. How are you going to give them back to me then? And maybe that is how my things have been taken care of.
MATRON:	Don't talk nonsense. Your things are perfectly safe. You must understand...
ROSEMARY:	Yes?
MATRON:	You must understand that, when the Court of Protection made out an order... what it meant was...
ROSEMARY:	That I am going to spend the rest of my life here. That is until, like Beryl, an ambulance carts me off to hospital to die.
MATRON:	Oh do stop talking about dying, Rosemary. You've got simply years and years ahead of you yet. But you must realise, the flat had to be emptied. The solicitors looking after your affairs had to empty the flat.
ROSEMARY:	Why?
MATRON:	Because everything has to be done through legal channels.
ROSEMARY:	So what has happened to my things? Why won't you tell me?
MATRON:	They've gone to the people you left them to.

ROSEMARY: But that was in my will!

MATRON: Yes.

ROSEMARY: But I'm still alive!

MATRON: Rosemary... you have no further need for what was in the flat. You couldn't move into The Grange lock, stock, and barrel. What has happened is that the solicitors wrote to all the people mentioned in your will who had been left bits and pieces...

ROSEMARY: That's all there was.

MATRON: What?

ROSEMARY: Bits and pieces.

MATRON: I didn't mean it to sound like that.

ROSEMARY: But it's true.

MATRON: I'm sure some of the bits are quite valuable and will be appreciated. Treasured. And that is not all there is. You know perfectly well there was some money left to you when your sister died.

ROSEMARY: She left it all to charity. She hated me.

MATRON: Fortunately for you she couldn't leave it all to charity even if she wanted to. Provision was made for you in your mother's will and your sister had to abide by that. So you see, the law is there to protect you. And you know that, so stop being so contrary. That money is in safe-keeping.

ROSEMARY: With this reputable firm of solicitors who have given away all my things.

MATRON: (*Losing patience.*) For the last time, Rosemary, and then, as far as I am concerned, the matter is closed. The people mentioned in your will had to affirm they would be prepared to look after your things, ensure their safekeeping until...

ROSEMARY: Say it. Go on, say it. Until I am dead.

MATRON: At which time the property would become legally theirs.

ROSEMARY: So that's it then.

MATRON: You wanted to know and I've told you.

ROSEMARY: All cut and dried. All legal and above board. I'm officially dead before I'm dead.

She goes back to her puzzle.

MATRON watches her for a moment and then turns to go. It is then that she sees the piece of paper on the floor. She bends down to retrieve it.

MATRON: What's this?

She straightens up, looking at the paper.

ROSEMARY: That's mine!

She stretches out to take it, a little too eagerly, pulling at it before MATRON has time to let it go and the paper rips. ROSEMARY stares in dismay at the piece in her hand. MATRON studies the piece in hers.

MATRON: What is it?

ROSEMARY: You tore it.

MATRON: I beg your pardon?

ROSEMARY: You tore it. I've had it all these years and you've torn it.

MATRON: On the contrary, Rosemary, it was you who tore it. If you hadn't snatched at it like that...

ROSEMARY: Give it to me. Give it to me!

MATRON: (*Handing the piece over.*) Calm down, Rosemary. Don't excite yourself like that.

ROSEMARY lays the pieces on the table, matching them up.

What is it anyway? Why is it so important?

ROSEMARY looks up and straight ahead, totally withdrawn.

MATRON picks up the two pieces of paper and glances quickly over the contents.

Oh... I see... well there's no great harm done, my dear. It can easily be mended. A bit of scotch tape across the back and it will be as good as new.

ROSEMARY: It will never be the same again.

MATRON: No one will ever know it's even been damaged. (*No response.*) Would you like me to do it for you? (*No response.*) You should have had this framed years ago. It's a jolly good review isn't it? (*No response.*) I tell you what, I've got an empty frame in my office, just the right size. We'll repair it and put it in the frame so no one will ever know. You could keep it on your bedside cabinet. It's one of those self-supporting frames, very nice, leather. Well, mock leather. Would you like that? (*No response.*) Well I'll do it anyway.

MATRON turns and goes. There is a moment and then...

ROSEMARY: It doesn't really matter anymore. What difference does it make anyhow?

There is the sound of ROBERT whistling "My Old Man Said Follow the Van" and he enters, followed by TRACEY. He is carrying a set of stepladders and TRACEY has a large box of Christmas decorations.

ROBERT: Hello, Rosemary, me little darlin'. How are you getting on with your puzzle?

He sets up the ladder and then, having had no response from ROSEMARY, turns to look at her.

Rosemary? (*He goes to her.*) Rosemary!

He looks at TRACEY who puts down the box, crosses over to ROSEMARY's other side and starts to take her pulse. ROBERT snaps his fingers in front of her face.

ROSEMARY: Don't snap your fingers, Robert. It's extremely rude.

ROBERT: Gordon Bennett, Rosemary! Don't do that to me. I thought you'd taken a turn and you almost gave me one. What are you up to?

ROSEMARY: I don't think I'm up to anything anymore, Robert.

ROBERT: What? (*He takes this in.*) Oh, come off it, I don't believe you.

ROSEMARY: Well it's true I'm afraid.

ROBERT: Don't say things like that, Rosemary. You don't really mean it.

ROSEMARY: Yes I do.

ROBERT: Well I still don't believe you. And Nurse Williams doesn't believe you either. Do you, nurse?

TRACEY: No.

ROBERT: So we'll have none of that nonsense. Christmas is coming, the goose is getting fat.

TRACEY & ROSEMARY: Please put a penny in the old man's hat.

ROBERT: And it wouldn't surprise me to see you dancing the can-can as your party piece.

ROSEMARY: Party piece?

ROBERT: Oh, everybody does a party piece.

TRACEY: Just don't ask him to do his, that's all.

ROBERT: Now come on, old gal, we're going to move you. You're in the way there.

ROSEMARY: Somehow it seems I've always been in the way.

ROBERT: Gordon Bennett! What's brought all this on? Do I sense a trough of deep depression lying over The Grange? A mood of black despair? Cheer up, you old trouper. Haven't you heard you're supposed to (*Singing.*) Look for the silver lining, when' ere a cloud appears in the blue. Now come on, let's be having you.

He takes one arm, TRACEY takes the other and they help ROSEMARY to her feet and to the chair ROBERT has already placed for her.

Don't you fall over now or matron will have our guts for garters. Are you still not using your frame?

ROSEMARY: Only when I must.

TRACEY: I do wish you'd use it, Rosemary. You're no featherweight you know.

ROSEMARY: Thank you.

TRACEY: And you could take a tumble with pretty nasty consequences.

ROSEMARY: Matron said I could have my sticks back.

TRACEY: Did she?

ROSEMARY: You didn't throw them away did you, Robert?

ROBERT: No, I kept them for you safe and sound.

TRACEY: Maybe we'd best check with matron first.

ROBERT: What for? If Rosemary says she can have her sticks, her sticks she will have.

ROSEMARY: Thank you, Robert.

ROBERT: (*Singing.*) Here comes the bride, all fat and wide... (*He takes a sprig of mistletoe from his pocket and holds it above them.*) Look up, Rosemary. What do you see?

She looks up and he kisses her cheek. ROSEMARY laughs. They seat her in the chair and ROBERT goes back for her table.

But I know who you'd rather be kissing.

TRACEY goes back to the box of decorations.

ROSEMARY: Who would I rather be kissing?

ROBERT: Shhhh... not a word... my lips are sealed. Look... Mm-mm-mm.

ROSEMARY: What?

ROBERT: (*Pulling extraordinary faces.*) Superglue.

ROSEMARY laughs.

ROBERT: See? I knew this fit of melancholia wouldn't last. Did anyone ever tell you what a wonderful smile you have?

ROSEMARY: Oh, Robert.

ROBERT: (*Looking at the puzzle.*) My word, you're getting on well with that.

TRACEY: And shouldn't we be getting on with this? (*She indicates the decorations which she has been busy sorting out*).

ROSEMARY: I'm having a bit of trouble with the blue bits.

ROBERT: Don't we all?

ROSEMARY: I mean, look at this silly piece. Where does that go?

ROBERT: (*Taking it from her and placing it.*) There.

ROSEMARY: Oh. (*Pause.*) Thank you, Robert.

ROBERT: (*Steps back from the chair and rolls up his sleeves.*) And now ze great illusionist, Roberto ze Remarkable, weezout a hat, weel produce no rabbeet, no pigeon, no goldfish in a bowl, but... ta-ra! (*He swings around and extends both arms.*) Walter!

WALTER appears, looks around.

WALTER: Christmas decorations. I like Christmas decorations.

ROBERT: We know you do, Walt. Last year you pulled them all down and took them to your room.

WALTER: Did I, Mr Benham? I don't remember that.

TRACEY: Come and sit down, Walter, and watch us putting them up.

WALTER: I want to help.

ROSEMARY: Come and sit next to me, Walter.

ROBERT: Ho ho ho! Did you hear that imperious summons, Walter baby? (*He leans right into him.*) Give in with good grace now but later... (*He taps the side of his nose.*) ...show her who wears the pants.

TRACEY: Huh!

WALTER: No, I want to help you, Mr Benham. I'll hold the ladder.

ROBERT: Walter, what's the matter with you, man? You've had your marching orders, now march.

He places his hands on WALTER's shoulders and marches him to the chair beside ROSEMARY where he forces him down.

WALTER: But...

ROBERT: (*Pushing him down again.*) But me no buts. I want to hold the ladder.

TRACEY: Who's holding the ladder?

ROBERT: I am. You're going up it. We'll start here. (*By the windows.*)

TRACEY: Why am I going up the ladder?

ROBERT: Because, if you fall, I will be in a position to catch you. Whereas, if I fall, there'd be no one in a position to catch me. Now is that logical or isn't it. Walter, I arsks ya, is that logical?

WALTER: No, Mr Benham.

ROBERT: What?

WALTER: If I was to hold the ladder, hold it you see, and you were to fall, I could let go the ladder and catch you.

ROBERT: Forget it, mate, forget it. (*He holds out a streamer to TRACEY.*) Here, cop hold of that.

WALTER starts to rise.

Not you, Walter, sit down.

WALTER sits. They start to put up the decorations.

ROSEMARY: Matron tore up my review.

WALTER: Your what?

ROSEMARY: My review. You know... My review! In the paper... I read it to you.

WALTER: Read it to me again.

ROSEMARY: I haven't got it anymore. She took it away.

WALTER: What for?

ROSEMARY: Said she was going to fix it. She won't of course. People never do what they say they're going to do.

WALTER: I do.

ROSEMARY: You're the exception that proves the rule.

WALTER: What rule?

ROSEMARY: It's a saying.

WALTER: What is?

ROSEMARY: Walter, are you having one of your off days?

WALTER: Half and half.

ROSEMARY: What does that mean?

WALTER: Not as good as I could be.

ROSEMARY: Why ever not?

WALTER: Nervous. It's because I'm nervous.

ROSEMARY: Oh, Walter... (*She places a hand on his.*) ...whatever's made you nervous?

WALTER: Christmas is coming.

ROSEMARY: Don't you like Christmas? Whoever heard of anyone not liking Christmas? It's a celebration. The time when we celebrate the birth of our Lord. That dear little boy child laying in the manger.

WALTER: Meek and mild.

ROSEMARY: It's a time for joy, Walter.

ROBERT;   Did you know her, Walt?

WALTER: Who, Mr Benham?

ROBERT: Joy.

ROSEMARY: Ignore him. Tell me why you're nervous.

WALTER: Because... because... I don't know... how you will like the present.

ROSEMARY: Present? You got me a Christmas present?

WALTER: (*Nodding.*) Do you want to see it?

ROSEMARY: No, of course not. Don't be silly, Walter. You're not supposed to give Christmas presents till Christmas day.

WALTER: Yes, but...

ROSEMARY: Don't look now, Walter, but they're at it again.

WALTER: Hey? (*He turns to look.*)

ROSEMARY: See? He's got his hand on her leg. High up.

WALTER: Hey! You're at it again, aren't you? You're at it!

ROBERT: Having a great time, Walt.

ROSEMARY: Shush, Walter. Ignore them. They're only showing off.

WALTER: About this present...

ROSEMARY: I haven't got you one.

WALTER: What?

ROSEMARY: No. I haven't even begun to think about Christmas yet. But there's still time, isn't there? I've still time. How many shopping days left to Christmas?

WALTER: I don't know.

ROSEMARY: Robert? How many shopping days are there to Christmas?

ROBERT: Twelve, Rosemary dear, twelve shopping days. Hey, Walter! Feel like singing?

WALTER: No thank you, Mr Benham.

ROBERT: Oh, come on. I know you know the words. (*Singing.*) On the first day of Christmas my true love gave to me, a partridge in a pear tree.

TRACEY: (*Gives a shriek.*) Hold the ladder! Hold the ladder!

ROBERT: (*Grabbing it.*) Sorry... sorry.

WALTER: About this present...

ROSEMARY: I'd be careful if I were you, nurse Williams. You could take a nasty tumble with disastrous consequences.

TRACEY: Thank you, Rosemary, I'll bear your... (*She slaps ROBERT's hand.*) ...warning in mind.

WALTER: About this present...

There is another shriek from TRACEY. WALTER and ROSEMARY both turn to look.

TRACEY: Look, Mr "hands everywhere" Benham, if you don't lay off I'm coming down and you can do the lot be yourself, all right? You're worse than a bloody octopus.

ROSEMARY: Language!

TRACEY: There's a time and place for everything you know.

ROBERT raises two placating hands. ROSEMARY and WALTER turn back.

WALTER: About this present...

ROSEMARY: What, Walter?

WALTER: About this present...

ROSEMARY: Are we going to have a tree, Robert?

ROBERT: Of course. We always have a tree. It goes right here.

ROSEMARY: With candles?

ROBERT: Candles? You mean real, flaming, old-fashioned candles? Real light - up - with - matches type candles? Made of wax that melts and runs everywhere?

ROSEMARY: Of course that's what I mean. When I was little we always had candles on our tree.

ROBERT: That's because electricity hadn't been invented yet, Rosemary.

WALTER: About this present...

ROBERT: These days we have flashers. You know, now you see 'em, now you don't. (*He opens and closes his coat in quick succession.*)

ROSEMARY: That man can be SO disgusting.

WALTER: Don't take any notice.

ROSEMARY: Oh, I won't. The best thing to do with disgusting people is simply ignore them.

WALTER: About this present...

MATRON enters carrying the framed review.

MATRON: (*Brightly to ROBERT and TRACEY.*) Hello! How are you two getting on?

WALTER: They're always getting on.

MATRON: And how are you two getting on?

WALTER: I want to tell Rosemary about...

ROSEMARY: I was just talking about the little candles we used to have on our Christmas tree when I was a girl. Like barley-sugar twists. I remember I used to sit for, oh, ages and ages, just sit gazing at them. Such a pretty light they gave. And then daddy would put our presents under the tree.

WALTER: About this present...

MATRON: (*Holding out the frame.*) Here you are, Rosemary, as good as ever it was and in such a smart frame.

ROSEMARY takes the frame. WALTER gets to his feet.

WALTER: ABOUT THIS PRESENT!!!

Everyone stares at him in shocked silence.

MATRON: I beg your pardon, Walter. And what was all that about?

WALTER: Nothing... nothing... (*He turns away.*)

MATRON: Well, if it was nothing, you certainly made enough fuss about it. We'll have a little less of that kind of thing if you don't mind. Well, Rosemary? Do you like it?

ROSEMARY: (*She hugs the frame but is staring at WALTER.*) It's very nice. Thank you.

MATRON: Good. (*She turns and stalks out.*)

ROSEMARY: Come and sit by me, Walter.

WALTER returns to his chair.

Look, it's been framed.

WALTER: Do you like angels, Rosemary?

ROSEMARY: What?

WALTER: Angels. Do you like 'em?

ROSEMARY: Well of course I do. Everybody does. Angels? All congregated around the throne of God on high. Singing His praises. Angels and archangels, seraphim and cherubim, beautiful creatures, shining creatures with radiant faces.

WALTER: Is that what heaven is like?

ROSEMARY: Yes, that must be what heaven is like.

ROBERT: Just like a telly commercial, Walt.

ROSEMARY: He'll never see it though, carrying on the way he does. (*Suddenly suspicious.*) Why do you ask me that?

WALTER: What?

ROSEMARY: About angels.

WALTER: I was just wondering.

ROSEMARY: Funny question to ask.

WALTER: No it's not. It's Christmas nearly.

ROSEMARY: (*Still suspicious.*) And that reminded you of angels?

WALTER: Yes. And the angel of the Lord came down.

ROSEMARY: And said peace on earth, goodwill to all men.

ROBERT: (*Passing by, moving the ladder to another position.*) That's what the man said.

ROSEMARY: Not man, Robert. Angel.

ROBERT: The part of us that isn't animal, hey, Walter? Right, my turn up the ladder.

He shins nimbly up and TRACEY hands him the end of a streamer.

ROSEMARY: Very pretty.

ROBERT: Thank you, Rosemary. I'm glad you approve.

ROSEMARY: (*Returns to her puzzle.*) Look, Walter, it's nearly finished. Just a small patch here... and here...and a little bit here... (*Holding up a piece.*) ...Let me see now.

WALTER: It was Christmas when my wife left me.

ROSEMARY: (*Looking up sharply.*) What?

WALTER: My wife.

ROSEMARY: Wife?

WALTER: She left me. It was Christmas.

ROSEMARY: I didn't know you were married.

WALTER: Yes, I was... married... once. I was married all right. Well and truly married. Yes. But she's dead now. Isn't she, Mr Benham?

ROBERT: What?

WALTER: She's dead. My wife. She's dead.

ROBERT: Yes.

WALTER: You see?

ROSEMARY: I didn't disbelieve you, Walter. I am sorry. Is that what you mean when you say she left you?

WALTER: No. She walked out. Just walked out. I came home, the Christmas tree lights all lit up, all the lights in the house on, and she was gone. Just gone. Taken the boys and gone.

ROSEMARY: Oh.

WALTER: I opened the door... so quietly... shhh...Christmas presents... I had Christmas presents with me. I sneaked into the house so no one would know I was there. Into the house to hide them before anyone could see. I didn't know there was no one else there, in the house I mean. I hid the presents under the stairs right far back, in the dark, and then I went into the living room, and then into the dining room, and then into the kitchen. And then I went upstairs and into the bedroom all pink and cream. Then into the boys' bedroom, and then into the bathroom and the lavvy, black and white.

And then I went down the stairs again, then into the garden, then into the street, looked this way, that way, Then back into the house, into all the rooms, and into the back garden and then I sort of sat down like I had no legs and I was sick. I was sick all over my front. I just went on being sick and then I sort of rolled over like I had died. And I could see the Christmas tree lights, all blurred like, I could see them through the window and... and...

Silence.

ROSEMARY: And what, Walter?

WALTER: I don't remember. (*Pause.*) But she's dead now.

ROSEMARY: What about your boys?

WALTER: Boys?

ROSEMARY: You said you had boys.

WALTER shrugs. Silence.

WALTER: Were you married, Rosemary?

ROSEMARY: Walter, you know I was never married. I'm Miss Davis not Mrs. You know that.

WALTER: Did you never think about it?

ROSEMARY: Well of course I thought about it. It's not that I didn't want to get married. The opportunity just never arose that's all.

WALTER: How come?

ROSEMARY: I don't know. Who knows? It wasn't meant to be I suppose. Not everyone in this world gets married,

	do they? Even when they want to be.
WALTER:	That's true. Queen Elizabeth never got married.
ROSEMARY:	The first you mean. Not our current queen.
WALTER:	The Virgin Queen they called her.
ROSEMARY:	Walter…
WALTER:	I bet she wasn't though.
ROSEMARY:	Walter!
WALTER:	What?
ROSEMARY:	You're getting as bad as he is.
WALTER:	Dinner time soon. I wonder what's for dinner.
ROSEMARY:	What's to-day?
WALTER:	Friday.
ROSEMARY:	Well that's it then. It's fish. Fish Fridays. And chips.
WALTER:	I like a good bit of fish.
ROBERT:	(*Moving to another spot.*) We all like a good bit of fish now and again, Walt.
ROSEMARY:	Mr Benham, when we wish you to join this conversation you will be invited to do so.
ROBERT:	Oh, pardon me, I'm sure.
ROSEMARY:	Sometimes the young do have to be put in their place.
WALTER:	Yes. You would have made a good mother,

Rosemary.

ROSEMARY: Walter! If you're going to continue in this vein I am going to have to leave. Oh, by the way, matron says I can have my sticks back. Robert's going to get them for me. Robert?

ROBERT: Is this an invitation to join the party?

ROSEMARY: Where are my sticks?

ROBERT: I'm busy right now, Rosemary. Do you really need them?

ROSEMARY: No, I suppose not. If I have to move I can ask Walter for assistance. I can lean on Walter.

WALTER: Yes, you can. You can do that. You can lean on me, Rosemary. I'd like that.

ROSEMARY: Walter!

WALTER: No fear of falling over, not with me holding you up.

ROSEMARY: Life is like a jigsaw puzzle isn't it? The only trouble is we're not given a picture on the box to show us how it should turn out.

ROBERT: My, Rosemary! What a wonderful philosophical thought. Worthy of Plato that is. I bet he would have come up with that one if they'd had jigsaws in ancient Greece.

WALTER: There was a racehorse called Plato once. Plato something. Or something Plato. I forget.

ROBERT: Walter, I am extremely dubious about the integrity of a tax inspector whose friends keep greyhounds and who knows the names of racehorses. Were you

	a gambling man?
WALTER:	I don't remember.
ROSEMARY:	(*Resenting the interruption.*) Where's the tree?
ROBERT:	All in good time, Rosemary. We've got to finish this lot first.
ROSEMARY:	Well why don't you get on with it then?
WALTER:	Get on with it.
ROSEMARY:	It will be dinner time soon.
WALTER:	Dinner time.
ROSEMARY:	If you did more and talked less you might achieve something worthwhile.
WALTER:	Worthwhile.
ROBERT:	The ex-champ, desperate to make his come-back, is once again totally demoralised by the dexterity of his opponent. Knocked senseless by a sudden flurry of hammer-like blows, his seconds throw in the towel.

He reels back to his decorating.

ROSEMARY:	Talk, talk, talk, talk, talk, talk, talk, and most of it nonsense. Show-off and nonsense.
WALTER:	It's not all talk, no. There's the other thing... you know... he's at it all the time. Never stops. Like a rabbit.
ROSEMARY:	I knew someone just like that once, as far as the talk goes I mean.

WALTER: Some people have it.

ROSEMARY: Have what?

WALTER: Gift of the gab.

ROSEMARY: This one certainly did. When I turned twenty-one I came into a little money. Well it was more than a little in those days. Nowadays, of course, it wouldn't buy a pig in a poke. It was from my grandfather, a legacy from his estate.

WALTER: Did he pay his death duties?

ROSEMARY: Walter. Can't you forget for one moment that you were a tax man? You should have left all that behind you. I know that in this life nothing is certain but death and taxes, I've heard that saying. The clever Mr Disraeli said that.

WALTER: No. Oh no no no no. No it wasn't. It was Mr Franklin.

ROSEMARY: I'm sorry, my dear, I don't like to contradict, but...

WALTER: I know! I know! I had it hanging up in my office. And it was signed, "Benjamin Franklin".

ROSEMARY: He signed it personally of course.

WALTER: I don't think so. I think it was one of the office juniors, for a joke like.

ROSEMARY: Oh, well, that explains it then. If it was one of the office juniors, one of the know-it-all brigade... (*This loud enough for ROBERT's benefit.*) ...he made a mistake.

WALTER: You think so?

ROSEMARY: I know so.

WALTER: And all these years here I've been thinking it was Benjamin Franklin.

ROSEMARY: We all make mistakes in life, Walter.

ROBERT: It's all right, Walt, "Land Of Hope And Glory" was written by that clever Mr Wagner. Even I was floored by that one.

ROSEMARY: As I was saying, before that rude interruption, when I was left the money I had only just attained my majority and I was very... naive. And there was a young actor I knew who persuaded me to start this theatre company on the south coast. I shouldn't have done it of course. It was a silly thing to do, I can see that now. But I was young, younger than my years and I didn't know any better at the time. And he was so charming. And how he could talk! My money all went of course. And so did he. A big agent came down to see him, for reasons we won't discuss, and when the season was over and we were back in London I never saw him again, except accidentally and then he avoided me. He became a big name, a star, and it was I who gave him his first chance. I still have his photograph. Oh, no, I don't. It was in my bureau and my bureau's gone. What has happened to all my papers? My photographs? Who is peeping at my personal things? I must ask matron.

WALTER: Would I know him?

ROSEMARY: Hmn? Oh, yes. Yes, you would know him all right. Everyone knows him. He's a household name. Theatre, films, television, radio, you name it, he's done it. What people don't know of course is that he drinks. A hopeless alcoholic. Really. So his looks have gone. Sad. Drink does that to people. And he's old now of course. In the photograph he's still only twenty and quite attractive in a pixyish sort of way. There was no chance of him marrying me though.

WALTER: Why was that?

ROSEMARY: He didn't like women.

WALTER: Why was that?

ROSEMARY: What I mean is... well, he didn't like women... that way. Some men don't you know.

WALTER: Yes.

ROSEMARY: But I didn't know anything about things like that then. In those days it was a secret. You didn't shout it from the rooftops like they do today. Of course we never did anything. In those days you weren't supposed to. And I was glad because I didn't want to. I believed in waiting till you were married. Marriage is a sacred state ordained by God. So it never occurred to me he didn't want it either, for different reasons. A peck on the cheek, holding hands sometimes, that was all. I was so in love though. But it was a long time ago.

WALTER: Did you never meet anybody else?

ROSEMARY: Well, only a few years ago, I met this very nice man. He was a sidesman at the church and a widower. No children. But he had been married for thirty years before his wife passed away so you could tell he was stable. I think he was going to make a proposal. In fact I know he was. Everything was pointing in that direction. Then, one day, he died. Just like that. No warning. Nothing. Just died.

WALTER: Oh.

Silence. ROBERT and TRACEY go out with the ladder and box.

Never mind, Rosemary, you've got me now.

ROSEMARY: What's that, Walter?

WALTER: You've got me now. We're good friends. You and me. Friends.

ROSEMARY: Yes. Yes we are. There's just one thing, Walter...

WALTER frowns, expecting the worst.

I would appreciate it if you would stop telling everyone about my being an actress.

WALTER: But you are. You are an actress.

ROSEMARY: (*Shakes her head.*) No, Walter. The theatre never loved me as I loved it. Oh, I had dreams, I had hopes, especially after this... (*She looks at the review.*) ...some people are born stars, others are made stars, some have stardom thrust upon them. That's a quote, you know. But, for me, it never happened. It never even really started. Not even bit parts on television, Walter, just walk-ons, just one of the crowd. (*She gazes at the review then holds it out to him.*) You have this, Walter. I'd like you to have it.

He takes it.

Even the walk-ons were few and far between. Very few and very far between.

ROBERT: (*Off.*) All right, Rosemary? Walter? I hope you're ready for this. Here we come! Ta-ra!

ROBERT and TRACEY appear with the Christmas tree already decorated and ready to be put in position.

TRACEY: How do you like it?

ROBERT: Sorry there's no real light-up candles for you, Rosemary?

TRACEY: And we seem to have lost the Christmas tree fairy. Can't find her anywhere. She should be up there, right on top. You haven't got her have you, Walter?

WALTER shakes his head.

ROSEMARY: She's gone AWOL, the naughty girl.

TRACEY: Gone what?

ROSEMARY: Absent without leave. AWOL. That's what we used to say during the war, in the WACS.

WALTER: We used to say it too, in the men's section.

ROBERT: Men's section of what, Walter?

WALTER: The army of course. You can be really dense sometimes, Mr Benham.

ROBERT: I know, Walter. You've just got to be patient with me, old son. (*He has plugged in the lights.*) Right, everybody ready? Blackpool, eat your heart out. And now, ze great Roberto, Roberto ze magnifique, he proudly present ze sensation of ze century...

WALTER: Get on with it, for Christ's sake.

ROSEMARY: Walter!

ROBERT: Ta-ra!

He flicks the switch. There is a concerted groan of disappointment, a silence, then...

WALTER: Nothing happened, Mr Benham.

BLACKOUT.

SCENE THREE

CHORUS: Put on your ta-ta, little girlie, Do do what I want you to,
Far from the busy hurly-burly, I've got lots to say to you,
My head's completely twirly-whirly, my girl I want you to be,
So put on your ta-ta, your pretty little ta-ta, and come out a ta-ta with me.

The CHRISTMAS TREE LIGHTS come up and then LIGHTS UP. It is Christmas Eve.

ROBERT is admiring the Christmas tree. He makes a couple of adjustments. MATRON enters from the hall. He stops what he is doing and turns to see her.

ROBERT: Will she be all right? What did the doctor say?

MATRON: He doesn't seem unduly concerned.

ROBERT: I don't know, matron, it was a pretty nasty fall. Maybe she really ought to go to hospital for observation. She didn't break anything I know but...

MATRON: But I think doctor knows best, Robert, so let's abide by his decision shall we? If doctor felt she should be in hospital then that's where she would be. I know the bruises look pretty nasty but then some people do bruise very easily. All things considered she seems jolly cheerful to me. We might even have her up and about tomorrow for Christmas dinner. (*She turns to go, stops, turns back.*) Oh, and by the way, Robert, I've been meaning for some time now to have a serious word with you.

ROBERT: About what, matron?

MATRON: I think you know about what. (*Clearing her throat.*) I'm not usually one to beat about the bush, as you know, but... well... rumours have reached my ears that... that your behaviour with a certain young member of the nursing staff is... how shall I put this?

ROBERT: Carefully?

MATRON: What?

ROBERT: Nothing.

MATRON: ...Is a little indiscreet?... ah... flamboyant?

ROBERT: That's careful.

MATRON: What?

ROBERT: I said, I'm glad she's cheerful.

MATRON: Who?

ROBERT: Rosemary.

MATRON: We are no longer discussing Rosemary. We are discussing your conduct and a very serious matter. I do wish you wouldn't be so flippant, Robert. We all know you have a way with words but changing the subject won't divert me. Now I can't, and have no wish to interfere in private matters. But, for the sake of decency and appearances, private matters should be kept private. Do I make myself clear? If

>   this matter is brought to my attention again I will be forced into the position of having to take steps to terminate your contract of employment. I am sorry to mention this on Christmas Eve but that's the way it is.

ROBERT: May I enquire where these rumours came from?

MATRON: You may. (*Pause.*) Robert, I do wish you'd give up smoking, you smell like a brass ashtray. (*Going.*) I don't know how she puts up with it.

ROBERT: Was it Walter?

MATRON: No, it wasn't. In Walter's eyes, it seems, you can do no wrong. But in my eyes, Mr Benham, you can. So please heed my warning.

ROBERT: Yes, matron.

And she has gone.

> And a merry Christmas to you too.

He goes back to the tree. TRACEY enters.

TRACEY: Matron's just passed me with a face like a hatchet. What's up?

ROBERT: She's been giving me another lecture.

TRACEY: About what?

ROBERT: You.

TRACEY: Oh.

ROBERT: You, me, the birds, and the bees.

TRACEY: What did she say?

ROBERT: It's okay. Relax. The blame was laid entirely on my broad, masculine shoulders. My behaviour was railed against, not yours. Matron is quaintly old-fashioned.

TRACEY: How's Rosemary? Did she say?

ROBERT: According to the medical profession Rosemary is in peak condition for the decathlon.

TRACEY: Well she must be getting better. She wouldn't let me help with the puzzle. I showed her where a piece went and got my wrist slapped.

ROBERT: So that makes two of us. I'll be getting my cards.

TRACEY: Is that what she said?

ROBERT: Threatened. But it's got to come. So... (*He takes her in his arms.*) ...shall we have the last waltz? Before our world disintegrates

He starts to lead her in a waltz.

ROSEMARY appears and stands watching them. She is in dressing gown and furry mules and is using her sticks. ROBERT sees her and stops dancing.

Rosemary!

ROSEMARY: You're at it again I see.

TRACEY: (*Going to her.*) What are you doing out of bed?

ROBERT: Going AWOL, Rosemary?

TRACEY: Now come along, back to your room at once.

ROSEMARY: No, please... I want to sit up for a while.

TRACEY: Rosemary...

ROSEMARY: It's lonely in there.

TRACEY: Matron will be furious.

ROBERT: Who cares? (*He takes ROSEMARY's other arm.*) Come on, old girl.

TRACEY: Robert...

ROBERT: I'll take the blame. Lay it all on me.

TRACEY: She should be in bed.

ROBERT: She should be where she wants to be. What are you, a socialist or something? Always telling people what's best for them. (*They put ROSEMARY in a chair.*) There... comfy?

ROSEMARY: Thank you, Robert. I can look at the tree. You got it to work then. But you didn't find the fairy.

ROBERT: Nope, not a sign of her.

ROSEMARY: Naughty girl. I wonder where she's got to.

ROBERT: Maybe Walter did take a secret shine to her though a raid on his room failed to uncover any evidence. Talk of the devil...why do I open my big mouth?

WALTER appears. ROBERT places a chair for him next to ROSEMARY.

Here you are, Walter. Nurse Williams? Why don't you and I retire to the nearest broom cupboard?

ROSEMARY: Oh, Robert, I despair for you, I really do. How can you carry on the way you do?

ROBERT: Very easily, Rosemary.

ROSEMARY: There will be tears before bedtime, mark my words. One of these days, Robert, one of these days, when you decide to grow up, you will find out what love is all about, really about.

ROBERT: Maybe you're right there, Rosemary. Walter, are you going to sit down or aren't you?

WALTER advances on the chair.

ROSEMARY: I hope I am, for your sake. Remember my words.

ROBERT: I will.

WALTER sits. He is clutching the framed review.

And I tell you what, having had two lectures in as many minutes, and feeling totally deflated, we won't retire to the broom cupboard.

ROSEMARY: Good.

ROBERT: We'll retire to the kitchen for a quick tongue sandwich instead. (*To TRACEY.*) Fancy it?

TRACEY: Well I certainly don't want to be in here when matron comes by. And the kitchen is as good a place as any in which to be busy.

ROBERT: And what busy little bees we shall be, making lots and lots of honey, yum yum.

And they have gone.

WALTER: I'd like some honey. It's a long time since I had honey. Can't remember the last time I had honey. We had mince for dinner. I'm not too partial to mince. Never know what's in it. Tomorrow's turkey of course. Turkey and Christmas pudding. Now I like a bit of Christmas pudding. I'm glad you're feeling better, Rosemary.

ROSEMARY: I don't feel better.

WALTER: Oh. (*Pause.*) But you're up!

ROSEMARY: I'm up but I don't feel better.

WALTER: Oh. (*Pause.*) Then why are you up?

ROSEMARY: Because if I stayed in bed I'd feel worse.

WALTER: Oh. (*Pause.*) Did you have mince for dinner?

ROSEMARY: No, I had some soup, some kind of soup, brown soup. I don't know what it was.

WALTER: Probably some of the gravy from the mince.

ROSEMARY: Yes, I didn't eat much.

WALTER: You'll eat more to-morrow, when it's turkey.

ROSEMARY: I didn't get you a Christmas present, Walter.

WALTER: Hey? Oh, that's all right.

ROSEMARY: I meant to. A real present I mean. But then I had this fall and I wasn't able to go out and get one for you, choose it personally, you know. I could have got someone else to do it for me but then I had this fall and that put it right out of my head.

WALTER: That's all right, Rosemary.

ROSEMARY: I did so want to get you something really nice for Christmas but the fall put it right out of my head.

            When did you last go out, Walter?

WALTER: Out of my head?

ROSEMARY: No, you silly thing! Out of here. Out of here.

WALTER: Here?

ROSEMARY: Yes, out of here, into the street, outside.

WALTER: Outside? Oh, a long time ago. I don't remember. But it was a long time ago. I couldn't go out now though. Oh, no, not now. No, I'd be frightened to go out now. It's dangerous out there. I'd get lost and I wouldn't be able to find my way back. No, I couldn't go out there now. Oh, no, definitely not. No.

ROSEMARY: I'm sure you could if you really wanted to,

WALTER shakes his head violently.

            I would. I want to. I want to go home.

WALTER: Home?

ROSEMARY: To my flat.

WALTER: I'd go if you went, Rosemary.

ROSEMARY: Only it's all empty now.

WALTER: I'd go if I was with you. We could go together. I wouldn't be afraid then. And you could lean on me so that you didn't fall down. That would be nice don't you think? Wouldn't you like that? I tell you what, we could get married. We could go and live in your flat together, just you and me.

Silence.

ROSEMARY: You're asking me to marry you, Walter?

WALTER: Yes. (*Pause.*) It was Mr Benham suggested it. (*Pause.*) But I don't mind... if we got married I mean.

ROSEMARY: Where would we have the wedding?

WALTER: Here.

ROSEMARY: I always wanted a church wedding.

WALTER: Mr Benham could be best man. He'd like that.

ROSEMARY: And nurse Williams could be a bridesmaid.

WALTER: A bridesmaid.

ROSEMARY: But who would give me away? The bride has to be given away.

WALTER: Mr Putnam could do that.

ROSEMARY: Pity about poor Beryl.

WALTER: She'll miss it.

ROSEMARY: She could have been maid of honour.

WALTER: Matron.

ROSEMARY: (*Suddenly brought down to earth.*) It's too late, Walter.

WALTER: Never!

ROSEMARY: Yes, it is. Too late. I'm glad you asked me, my dear.

Thank you. That has made me very happy. But it's too late. We couldn't live in my flat you see because it's empty. There's nothing there. It's all gone. Been given away. There's nothing left. I don't have anything left.

WALTER: Except me. You've got me.

ROSEMARY: Yes, I've got you.

WALTER gets to his feet, puts the frame in ROSEMARY's lap, and starts to go.

Where are you going?

WALTER: Stay there, Rosemary. Don't you move. I'm going to fetch your Christmas present.

ROSEMARY: Not till tomorrow, Walter.

WALTER: No, no, I can't wait. I want you to see it. I want you to have it now. I've got to give it to you now.

He has gone.

ROSEMARY sits, staring at the Christmas tree lights. She is smiling. She looks down at the review and her lips move as she silently reads her notice. There is the SOUND of APPLAUSE. ROSEMARY puts the review on the table and struggles to her feet. She faces out front and curtsies a couple of time. Then she falls back into the chair and, still smiling, goes back to staring at the lights. Then she turns out front, her eyes close and slowly, almost imperceptibly, her head falls forward.

There is a long moment and then ROBERT enters with two cups of tea.

ROBERT: Hello, hello? Where's our Walter then? Sent him

packing did you? Got a bit too boisterous did he? A bit too flamboyant? (*He puts down the cups.*) Rosemary? Are you asleep? I brought you a cup of tea. (*Silence.*) Rosemary? (*He knows but he doesn't want to believe it.*) Gordon Bennett, Rosemary, don't do this to me. (*He begins to break.*) Oh, Jesus!... Rosemary!... Rosemary! (*He pulls himself together.*) Where the hell is Walter?

WALTER enters carrying something. He stops when he sees ROBERT and the hand is whipped quickly behind his back.

WALTER: Oh! Mr Benham. What are you doing here?

ROBERT: I work here, Walter. I thought you knew that by now.

WALTER: Don't be cross with me, Mr Benham. I haven't done anything.

ROBERT: What have you got behind your back?

WALTER: Nothing!

ROBERT: (*Gently.*) Come on, Walter, come on.

WALTER: What's the matter, Mr Benham.

ROBERT: What have you got there, Walter? Is it the fairy?

WALTER: It's Rosemary's Christmas present. I made it for her.

ROBERT: Can I see it?

WALTER: You won't be cross with me, Mr Benham.

ROBERT: No, Walter, I won't be cross.

WALTER: (*Producing the present.*) Look, it's an angel. I carved it.

ROBERT: (*Takes the angel, starts to break again, half crying, half laughing.*) It's not very good, Walter, is it?

WALTER: It was the best I could do.

ROBERT: Yes, I know... I know... I'm sorry... sorry.

And now he really breaks.

WALTER: What's the matter, Mr Benham? What's the matter? Don't, Mr Benham! You're frightening me! Stop it!

ROBERT: We'll put it on top of the tree, Walter, your angel, right on top of the tree.

WALTER: Oh, no! No no no no. We can't do that. It's for Rosemary. It's for her. Rosemary must have it.

ROBERT: She's dead, Walter.

WALTER: (*Stares at him.*) You're not teasing me are you, Mr Benham?

ROBERT: No, I'm not teasing you, Walter.

WALTER: Oh. (*He looks at the angel.*) Am I too late then?

ROBERT: No, you're not too late. Go and give it to her.

He holds out the angel. WALTER looks at it, then back to ROBERT's face.

WALTER: You give it to her, Robert.

ROBERT turns away and places the angel in ROSEMARY's hands. When he turns back he sees that

WALTER is crying quietly. He goes back to him.

ROBERT: Don't, Walter. Don't take on... Please don't... Gordon Bennett, Walter... (*He takes WALTER in his arms and holds him tight, rocking him gently.*) Don't, Walter... please... don't... don't...

The LIGHTS FADE.

The CHRISTMAS TREE LIGHTS are the last to go.

www.ingramcontent.com/pod-product-compliance
Lightning Source LLC
Chambersburg PA
CBHW020011050426
42450CB00005B/413